THE GIFTS OF ADVERSITY

"*The Gifts of Adversity* shakes you and breaks t[...] you see life anew. The traumas of the Vietnar[...] to the U.S., bullying and racist experiences, [...] rible but transformative for this remarkable [...] clinical psychologist, wife, mother and extraordinary citizen-witness. This narrative makes one believe in the human capacity for enduring and transcending the worst that life puts humans through."

—ARTHUR KLEINMAN, MD
Professor of Psychiatry and Anthropology at Harvard University, author of *The Soul of Care*

"This excellent memoir is a treatise on resiliency. Refugees learn what people will do to each other and for each other. Dr. Tran tells of her personal traumas and of her quest for acceptance and healing. She demonstrates resilience by focusing on the heroic sacrifices, the kindness and the courage of the many people who helped her find a place in America. *The Gifts of Adversity* is a love song to diversity and an urgent call to action. Her story reminds us we are all deeply connected and need each other to flourish."

—MARY PIPHER, PhD
New York Times bestselling author of *Reviving Ophelia,*
Women Rowing North, and *The Middle of Everywhere*

"So often we wish away life's painful challenges. Yet Dr. Tran's courageous story illuminates the fact that the most difficult circumstances can awaken our resilience and reveal our indomitable human spirit. We discover how mindfulness and compassion can transform potential suffering into deep grace."

—TARA BRACH, PhD
author of *Radical Acceptance* and *Radical Compassion*

"*The Gifts of Adversity* is a moving, passionate, and inspiring memoir of survival, courage, and success by a Vietnamese refugee who became the first Vietnamese woman psychologist in America. It's a gift and a powerful illustration of how Dr. Tran transformed her adversities into hope, resilience, compassion, and acts of activism!"

—JEAN LAU CHIN, EdD, ABPP
Professor of Psychology at Adelphi University

"A story of transcendence, grit, and amazing grace. More than a "refugee story," Dr. Tran inspires and guides all of us who have faced trauma to cherish the good in ourselves, empower the strength we found to survive, so that we may boldly challenge that which is evil and unjust. Her story stirs hope and urges us to each embark on our own healing journey."

—SATSUKI INA, PhD
Professor Emeritus in the School of Education at California State University, Sacramento, psychotherapist, award-winning filmmaker, activist, and Japanese American internment camp survivor.

"*The Gifts of Adversity* is a timely book in the face of the #MeToo movement and the escalating anti-immigrants of color sentiment in our country. It is part self-help, part inspirational, part protest book, part textbook. All told with honesty, conviction, and a heartfelt desire to bringing awareness to the plight of refugees and immigrants while helping survivors of sexual abuse."

—HOANG CHI TRUONG
author of *TigerFish: A Memoir of a South Vietnamese Colonel's Daughter*

THE GIFTS OF
ADVERSITY

THE GIFTS OF
ADVERSITY

**Reflections of a Psychologist, Refugee,
and Survivor of Sexual Abuse**

CAROLEE GIAOUYEN TRAN, PhD

Bodhichitta
PRESS

Published by Bodhichitta Press

ISBN- 978-1-7346868-0-7 (Paperback)
ISBN- 978-1-7346868-1-4 (Ebook)

Bodhichitta
PRESS

Bodhichitta is a Sanskrit word that means enlightened mind.
It connotes a mind that strives towards awakening, compassion,
and ending suffering for the benefit of all sentient beings.

Cover design by Laura Duffy
Book design by Karen Minster

Printed in the United States of America

FIRST EDITION

www.caroleetran.com

A deep bow to my parents for their courage, perseverance, resilience, and for all they have given and sacrificed

———⊗⊗⊗———

*To my husband Ladson,
our daughters Carina and Mika,
and my siblings—my life's greatest gifts
and a constant reminder that
all things are possible*

Table of Contents

CONTENTS

April 29th, 1975

"Get up! Get up! It's time to go! Don't turn on the lights!"

My head was groggy and it spun with confusion. Seconds passed as I gradually recognized the voice of my maternal grandfather jolting me out of a deep sleep.

I tried to remember what they'd told me to do if this happened.

What? ... Oh yes.

I pushed myself up and staggered out of bed, then grabbed my small escape bag. Aunt Tuyet was already standing next to my bed, so I clutched her hand tightly. She was fourteen years old, and I was eight. My legs wobbled as I descended the steep set of stairs, which led to the front door. Looking out at our large glass window, I could see droves of people running in the street.

Oh no.

"I forgot my shoes," I cried out.

"Never mind," Grandfather said. "No time to go back."

I was forced to go barefoot into the streets. As soon as we stepped outside, I felt the earth under my feet first, and then the sensations of cement, asphalt, gravel, dirt, and lastly sand as we approached the ocean. We were swept along by a stampede of people running and panting in the dark. My heart was racing, and perspiration trickled down my back and forehead. Aunt Tuyet and I said nothing to each other as we ran, but I felt her sweaty fingers tightly gripping my hand.

Finally we arrived at the beach, hoping to board boats that would take us out to sea. But suddenly we saw soldiers and police officers with their guns lined up on the beach.

"Stop!" one of the officers barked at us loudly through the megaphone in his hand. "Go home. There is no reason to flee."

We all stopped in our tracks and stood there, stunned and confused.

"What are all of you doing here at this late hour?" the officer went on. "You need to go home and get some sleep. Everything is fine— you don't need to go anywhere."

The anxiety and tension of the adults surrounding me was as frightening as the soldiers. But gradually, my mom and grandparents huddled together and then turned around and waved for Aunt Tuyet and me to follow.

We returned home that night and I fell right back to sleep. The following early morning, I awoke to the sound of our little radio.

"Vietnam is now one united country!"

The South Vietnamese government had surrendered to the North Vietnamese communist troops. We in South Vietnam had lost the war, and the communists from North Vietnam had marched in and occupied Saigon.

My grandparents, mom, aunts, and uncles were all extremely agitated, my grandmother and aunts weeping openly. They were devastated by the loss of democratic Vietnam and what this meant for us personally.

My mom paced the floor and gathered our escape bags. She placed mine next to me. It contained one change of clothing, a toothbrush, and a picture of my family. My maternal grandfather kept looking out towards the ocean with his binoculars.

"There's a big ship out there," he announced to us loudly. "That is the ship that will take us out of Vietnam. We must board that ship as soon as possible!"

I rushed to the dining room table to eat my breakfast.

"Hurry up," Grandfather snapped. "Finish your breakfast!"

But I had lost my appetite. The bread in my mouth tasted like cardboard. Within minutes, I got up from the table, dumped most of my breakfast into the garbage can, and joined the adults standing in the living room. We said a quick prayer and then were off again, making our second attempt to escape.

We ran on foot, avoiding the beach and heading straight to the pier in hopes of getting aboard one of the fishing boats docked there, which would take us out to the big escape ship. This time I had my sandals on. My mom carried my three-year-old sister, NhaUyen, on her back, held there by a large sheet tied across my mom's chest. NhaUyen was unable to walk due to the second-degree burns on her legs from a gunpowder accident just five days earlier. My mom also carried ThyUyen, my fifteen-month-old sister, in a front pack, along with a small bag containing one outfit for each of them and several items of my dad's. He wasn't with us. He was stuck more than two hundred miles away, in Saigon.

For the final stretch of the run to the pier, we had to walk on wobbly, narrow wooden planks loosely placed above the ocean. I slipped and fell several times, almost plunging into the cold water below. Only Aunt Tuyet's firm grip on my hand saved me.

Once we arrived at the fishing boats, my mom showed one boat captain after another a large sack full of cash and pleaded for someone to take us out to sea. All of them shook their heads while smiling politely. A number of bystanders jeered and made fun of us.

"Go home ... Don't be fools ... Why are you trying to leave? Communism is great—we are all equal!"

Of course, these were South Vietnamese citizens who had never lived under the brutal and oppressive communist regime, as had many members of my family. They had no idea what was in store for them.

3

Finally, at around five o'clock, when the sun was not shining as brightly and my mother had become so desperate that she got down on her knees to beg for help, one fisherman agreed to take us out to the American ship. Our family quickly crowded onboard the fishing boat and headed out to sea.

I stood next to my mom on the vessel as she chanted softly, over and over again, "Jesus, Maria, Joseph, please keep us from harm. Jesus, Maria, Joseph, please save us from death." A steady stream of tears flowed from her eyes and glistened her flushed cheeks as we plowed up and down, heading out to sea.

As we approached the ship, I saw that many people had already boarded, while others were hanging off the sides, trying to climb aboard. Surrounding the ship were hundreds of smaller boats and a large scow that was directly connected to the ship. The only way to get onto the scow was to hop onto and out of the smaller boats, which formed a sort of bridge.

I was terrified. There were about twenty boats between us and the scow. I saw bodies floating in the water and people screaming for help as they fell and were smashed between boats.

"Jump!" Mom screamed at me, pushing and lifting me forward towards the scow.

After a while, I made it onto an elevated platform connected to the scow and looked down. I saw that the scow was packed with people, shoving and trampling on top of one another. Suitcases, purses, clothes, and dried goods were scattered everywhere among them. People yelled, screamed, begged, and cried in their frenzy and desperation to board the ship, trying to push their way to the front of the scow.

Then I heard an announcement from the ship's loudspeaker: "Everyone must remain calm. We will let women and children on first!"

Standing next to me, my mom yelled into my ear, "Hurry up—jump! You have to jump on right now!"

It was a life-or-death situation. Getting onto the scow was the only way to get aboard the rescue ship. I was petrified, but the alarm in my mom's voice and the fear in her eyes told me that I had no choice.

I jumped.

Once onboard I was completely separated from my family, buried at the bottom of the scow in a sea of people. I struggled to breathe, gasping for air as I was thrown around like a ragdoll. The crowding and shoving made it impossible for me to gain my footing. I became lightheaded and felt like I was about to pass out. Above me, men who were trying to get onto the ship were being kicked and thrown off the sides of the ship.

Suddenly, a man scooped me up into his arms, saying, "I'm taking you onboard." He carried me from the scow to the ship, and then disappeared.

Minutes later, I heard the ship's horn blow loudly. Initially I had no idea what it meant. Then I felt the ship moving. I walked gingerly to the edge of the deck to get a better look at what was happening. My fingers grasped so tightly onto the ship's rail that they began to ache.

From there I could see my six-year-old sister KimUyen below on a small fishing boat, along with my maternal grandparents and aunts. I looked for my mom, but she was nowhere to be found. My body shook uncontrollably, tears flooding my eyes, as I stood alone without a single member of my family. I reached out, hoping I could magically pull KimUyen onboard. But it was not to be. She got smaller and smaller as the ship pulled farther away. The distance between us became unreachable, unbearable! Suddenly, I felt all the energy leave my body. My legs weakened and buckled under me. I collapsed, curled into a ball, and covered my ears in an attempt to shut out the deafening screams and desperate wails surrounding me. It sounded like a torrential downpour of rain, but it was a booming orchestra of heartbreak, fear, and anguish, like none I had ever heard before. I was drowning in a sea of human suffering.

Even the faces of the American navy officers were red and wet with tears. I was alone and terrified, with no idea where this ship was taking me. I sobbed hysterically and rocked rhythmically back and forth as dusk fell, retreating inward and shutting out the rest of the world until the sky turned completely dark.

I escaped Vietnam on April 30th, 1975, the day my country fell to the communists. This book is about what happened after that day: the suffering and dislocation, the heartbreak and terror, but also my survival and journey to the United States. Now I am a Vietnamese American who has experienced and overcome multiple traumas. I have struggled, studied, earned a PhD, and now practice as a clinical psychologist who helps others heal from trauma.

This book is also about my family's experiences of acculturation in America and the multiple challenges we overcame. I hope our story will encourage greater understanding and compassion for refugees and immigrants. I felt compelled to write this book in light of the recent rise in anti-immigrant and refugee sentiment in this country, which has been deeply troubling to me.

Over the years, I've gained insights into how the many struggles of being a refugee and immigrant have given me some great gifts— what I refer to as "the gifts of adversity." My deepest impetus for writing this book is to be an instrument of hope and healing for others, as well as an advocate for greater compassion and understanding in this world, especially in the face of today's demonization of immigrants and refugees.

CHAPTER 1

In the Beginning

Let me begin with the story of my mother and her family.

My mother was the oldest of eleven children, and her family lived in North Vietnam. My grandfather worked as an interpreter for the French Navy and the interrogation unit in North Vietnam. He was fluent in French and English, having learned both languages between the ages of twelve and twenty, when he was a Catholic seminarian. But his involvement and work with the French made him and his family a target of suspicion to the Viet Minh. The Viet Minh, or League for Vietnamese Independence, had been formed by Ho Chi Minh in 1941 to liberate Vietnam from French colonial rule, and it had been waging an increasingly successful guerilla war against the French.

During the years leading up to the final confrontation between the Viet Minh and the French armies at Dien Bien Phu in 1954, the Viet Minh suspected my grandfather of being a spy for the French and had him under constant surveillance. As a result, my maternal grandfather was always on the run and rarely saw his family. This meant that my maternal grandmother was a single mother for the first nine years of my mom's life.

Whenever the fighting escalated between the French and the Viet Minh, my grandmother was forced to flee on foot with her children, without the help of her husband. The constant upheavals caused by the war and the need to find safe shelter were incredibly disruptive.

During the day, my mom watched her brother Khang, who was two years younger than her, and their infant sister Hanh, while my grandmother worked in the market. Though she was only about four years old, my mom recalls vividly how, each time bombs shook their house, she and her siblings had to take cover in the house's bomb shelter and hide there until the pounding and shaking stopped.

One evening, my grandfather boarded a small fishing boat that stopped at the edge of the town, Nho Quan, where my mom, then four-and-a-half, was sleeping in a small, modest house with her mother and siblings. My grandfather walked half a mile from the river to his house, dressed in brown pants, a tattered shirt, and a large hat.

He disguised himself as a beggar, but carried a backpack full of money to give to my grandmother. He only stayed for a few minutes to hand over the cash and give his wife instructions for the upcoming escape plan. He told her that she and the children might need to go into hiding in the forest again for several days, since he'd heard that the French army was planning to intensify the bombings and gunfire in their war against the Viet Minh.

"If any neighbors or French soldiers come to the house looking for the head of the household," he told my grandmother, "tell them you don't know where I am and fear that I've already been killed by the Viet Minh."

Shortly after my grandfather's secret visit, the French dropped more bombs than ever and flattened the market. Then more French troops invaded their town. My grandmother rushed home to find her three young children hiding in the bomb shelter. As the French troops and the fighting escalated and came closer to their home, they fled into the forest.

"I ran on foot with my mother," my mom told me, "while Khang and Hanh sat in two baskets hung on either end from a stick that my mother carried across her right shoulder. We saw people yelling and crying from their open wounds and dead bodies were everywhere. I especially felt bad for the crying babies who sat next to their dead mothers' bodies. Many French soldiers also raped our women and young girls in plain sight. These horrible scenes are forever seared into my memory."

My mom and grandmother ran along the railroad tracks for many miles, surrounded by loud gunfire and bombings. At one point, my mom fell and cut her left knee open, yet they could not stop to take care of her wound. They continued to run as blood seeped down her leg, turning it crimson.

"Don't stop to help anyone," my grandmother cried. "We have to keep going or the bombs will hit us!"

By the age of six, my mom had been displaced from her home three times, moving from Nho Quan to Phat Diem, then to Ha Noi, then to Hai Phong, and had witnessed many atrocities associated with the war. At times, she and her family endured prolonged periods of starvation and homelessness, being forced to hide in the forest to stay out of harm's way, and foraging for food there.

When my mom was six, however, they found safety in Hai Phong, which was outside the war zone, away from the bombing, soldiers, and fighting. While there, the family enjoyed three years of stability and relative prosperity. My grandfather continued to work as a translator for the French Navy and the interrogation unit, while my grandmother owned a profitable grocery store. My mom was sent off to an expensive French Catholic boarding school during those years, since that was what the wealthy did to give their children the opportunity to learn French language and culture.

My mom hated this school. The separation from her family made her extremely homesick. She also endured corporal punishment from the nuns, as well as food restrictions, constant infestations of lice, insufficient blankets during cold nights, and a regimented work schedule. Each young girl was assigned a "caretaker," usually an older female student. These caretakers were often mean and stole from their charges the beautiful handkerchiefs, good food, and other treats their parents sent.

My mom stayed at this boarding school until the age of nine. Shortly after her return from school, a historic event occurred. Between March and May of 1954, the Viet Minh battled and ultimately defeated the French armies at Dien Bien Phu. As a result, in July of 1954, the French reluctantly signed the Geneva Accords, which divided Vietnam (then known in the west as Indo-China) at the seventeenth parallel, separating the country into two separate regions: the communist North and the noncommunist South. This event marked the termination of the French colonization of Vietnam, after a hundred years, as well as France's direct influence in Southeast Asia.

My grandfather knew that the Viet Minh's victory made it more dangerous than ever for him and his family to remain in North Vietnam, which was now governed by the communist regime of Ho Chi Minh. They had to flee. Their fourth and final escape occurred in 1954, shortly after the Geneva Accords were signed.

My mom told me the story when she learned that I was writing this book:

My father had given us careful instructions. So late one night, my mom, four younger siblings, and I quietly walked a short distance to the river and boarded a boat. I was nine, Khang was seven, Hanh was five, Kim was three, and Quy was one year old. Father had told us to meet a fisherman at the pier, and he was there!

"Lie down flat," he whispered to us as he quickly draped blankets over us. He instructed us to go to sleep and not make any noise.

We had no trouble in the quiet night, moving slowly down the river, heading south. When we awoke in the morning, we boarded several busses, which eventually took us into South Vietnam. This escape was very peaceful compared to the other three. We did not have to dodge bombs, gunfire, or dead bodies along the way.

Once the family made it safely into the South, they reunited with my grandfather in Saigon. He found work at the American embassy as a structural engineer, and my grandmother opened another grocery store. By 1975, my mother's family was financially well off, and they enjoyed over twenty years of relative peace and stability.

My maternal grandfather, Hinh Sy Ho, and grandmother, Lieu Thi Ngo, in 1976.

My dad grew up in South Vietnam, in a Buddhist family. He was the second of eight siblings. While his family did experience some temporary dislocation for several days during the war, in comparison to my mom's family, they were far less exposed to the horrors of war, and they never lived under communism.

However, my dad did encounter some adversity. When he was three, his mother died in childbirth. But his father remarried and provided his children with a warm and loving home environment. My paternal grandfather had worked as a chef for wealthy French families in Saigon before the French left Vietnam. Afterwards he moved his family to Can Tho, where his older sister lived and had started a laundry service that became quite profitable.

When my dad attended high school, he moved back to Saigon to live with his older sister. Immediately after high school, my dad enlisted in the army, which was a requirement for all Vietnamese men. He was a brave, proud, and dedicated soldier and leader who served his country until the very end of the war. By 1975, my dad was a major in the South Vietnamese army. He encountered many adversities as he fought in the war and courageously led his soldiers on the battlefield against Ho Chi Minh's Viet Minh. On the rare occasions that he spoke about his service in the military, he told us that he'd come close to death several times. He was given many medals for his valor, and was even awarded an Army Commendation Medal in 1971 by the United States, presented to him by General Creighton Abrams.

CHAPTER 2

A Love Story

My parents' love story began in Saigon during July of 1961, when my dad came to visit a family friend who happened to live next door to my mom. He was twenty-one and had already been in the military for four years. She was sixteen years old.

My dad, Tam Thanh Tran, as a young officer, in 1962.
My mom, Hoa Thi Ho, during my parents' courtship, in 1962.

Each sat on their respective verandas, doing their own thing. My mom was taking care of her youngest brother, who was crying loudly. In an effort to help, my dad leaned over to her side of the railing and offered her five rambutans, a sweet, juicy tropical fruit with a white flesh.

"Hello, sister, would you like to give these to your brother? Maybe it will help him to stop crying." My mom was touched by his empathy and generosity. It also didn't hurt that he was handsome and exuded an air of kindness, sturdiness, and gentleness.

This was not the first time my parents had noticed one another. A week before, my mom had been standing on her veranda when she saw my dad walking on the street below. They made eye contact but didn't speak. So my mom was pleasantly surprised to see my dad leaning over the side of her veranda, offering her the rambutans.

A few days later, my dad wrote mom a letter and asked a neighbor girl to deliver it. In the letter he asked my mom if she would like to meet at a park to talk. My mom confessed that she skipped school for that first meeting. "I had to cut class to go, since there was no time after school. Every day, I was expected to go straight from school to my mom's grocery store to help her run it."

Additional "meetings" followed—at the movie theatre, the pho noodle shop, and sometimes at my maternal grandmother's grocery store. Each time they met they learned a little more about one another. My parents were wonderful complements for each other. My mom is passionate, energetic, competitive, ambitious, extroverted, and dramatic, while my dad was steady, calm, introverted, thoughtful, compassionate, and self-assured. My dad was really surprised when my mom easily polished off two bowls of noodle soup on her own on one of their dates. While he was amused and happy that she had a healthy appetite, he also worried whether he had enough money to pay the bill. Thankfully, my mom had brought her own money and could make up for what he was unable to pay.

These rendezvous went on for a year, until my mom's younger brother Khang discovered the love letters my dad had written to her.

He showed them to my maternal grandparents, who became enraged and ordered my mom to stop seeing my dad. My grandfather actually beat her after he read the love letters from my dad.

In spite of this punishment and restrictions imposed upon her, my mom couldn't bring herself to stop seeing my dad.

"I knew that I was truly in love with your dad when I could not stop thinking about him or seeing him, even if it meant receiving multiple beatings from my father. Every time I ate something, I wished your dad was there with me, so I could share it with him."

Unfortunately, my parents had little time to spend together, given my dad's frequent and lengthy deployments as a soldier. They really got to know each other through their written correspondences.

My dad's family was also against my parents dating.

At the time they were courting, people in North and South Vietnam harbored entrenched and negative stereotypes of each other. These stereotypes played an important role in creating the unwritten rule that Northerners and Southerners should not date or intermarry. Southerners viewed the Northerners as more formal, private, deliberative, and cultured to a degree that bordered on being arrogant. On the other hand, Northerners viewed the Southerners as being more casual, open, easygoing, and hedonistic to the point of not responsibly planning for the future.

These stereotypes were so deeply ingrained and powerful that they caused serious discrimination. For example, my mom speaks of enduring many incidents of bullying and discrimination by kids, teachers, and other adults after she and her family escaped into the South. She was teased for her accent and was beat up many times by other kids. She became known as the "tough girl from the North" because she fought back.

Her teachers also made derogatory comments about her during class. At times they also humiliated her by twisting her ears, pulling her hair, spanking her, or making her kneel in front of the class.

My grandparents on both sides were also disapproving of my parents' relationship because of their different religions, my mom being Catholic and my father a Buddhist. However, both families also practiced ancestor worship. Ancestor worship emphasizes the importance of honoring one's ancestors and recognizing that one's current existence and identity is connected to previous generations of elders. Polytheism is commonly practiced in Vietnam, so it is not unusual for families to practice two religions.

Even though my dad was raised Buddhist, he was also drawn to Catholicism during his time in the military. On the battlefield, he was often accompanied by Catholic chaplains, many of whom he grew to respect and admire. Unbeknownst to my mom and both sets of parents, my dad had independently solicited the guidance and instruction of these chaplains to teach him about the Catholic faith.

In the meantime, despite their parents' objections, my parents continued to secretly see each other and corresponded by mail for an additional two years. Then a significant event occurred that drastically changed the nature of my parents' relationship.

In early 1964, my dad's entire platoon perished in battle, except for him. On that day, he wrote in his journal:

A day of devastating loss and sadness! I keep thinking this is a nightmare. Within fifteen minutes, life and death was determined. All my platoon brothers have perished except for me. Without the help and the protection of God, I probably would have perished too. I would have been deprived of the opportunity to ever see my loved ones again. In escaping death, I feel like I was given a second chance at life.

This near-death experience caused my parents to realize that they no longer wanted to keep their relationship a secret. They knew that they loved each other and wanted to be able to date openly. They would tell their parents about my dad's close call and how it had crystalized their conviction to be together. With great trepidation, they each spoke to their parents. Thankfully, their parents listened to their wishes and allowed my mom and dad to see each other. My maternal grandparents were impressed to learn that my dad, on his own, had been learning about Catholicism and was seriously considering converting to their faith.

Several months later, with permission from her father, my mom was chaperoned by her younger brother Khang to travel a long distance to attend my father's baptism on the battlefield. In a journal entry dated December 20th, 1964, the day he was baptized into the Catholic Church, my dad recorded the immense joy and significance the day held for him:

> While the ceremony was simple, its meaning is profound, moving, and brings me great joy. Having my beloved here to witness my baptism is a gift that is priceless. Blessed Mother Mary, Jesus, and Heavenly Father, please watch over me and guide me to live according to your ways.

After a few more months had passed, my parents decided that they wanted to get married. They had been pleasantly surprised and grateful when their parents allowed them to date openly. Now, they hoped that their parents would be equally supportive of their desire to get married. While my dad's parents were not thrilled by the idea, they accepted his decision and gave their lukewarm blessing.

My mom's parents were far more reluctant and tried to discourage her from marrying my dad. Even though they liked him and thought he was a good person, they worried that his meager salary as a military officer would be insufficient to provide my mom with a financially comfortable life. They urged her to keep an open mind, consider other potential suitors, and "not settle." My grandparents also enlisted the assistance of one of my mom's first cousins, Father Ky, an ordained Franciscan priest, to "talk some sense" into her.

Father Ky set up a private meeting with my parents and asked them whether they truly loved each other.

"Yes," they each said, "without a doubt."

Father Ky went to my mom's parents and urged them to consent to my parents' request to marry. It worked. Shortly afterwards, my maternal grandparents sat down with my parents to give them permission. In that meeting, my grandfather emphasized that he and my grandmother were relenting because they did not want to be blamed for depriving my mom of the love of her life or her chance at happiness.

On August 21st, 1965, Father Ky was the celebrant for my parents' wedding at my mom's Catholic church in Saigon. Sadly, within a year, Father Ky was killed in a motorcycle accident. My parents were devastated and heartbroken by his sudden and premature death.

My parents on their wedding day in 1965, with Father Ky.

CHAPTER 3

Adversity and Perseverance

In the late afternoon on a weekday in June of 1967, when I was eight months old, my cheeks started blushing bright red and my forehead felt hot to the touch. My mom says I was lethargic, staring into space with glazed eyes. My arms and legs were floppy and limp—motionless deadweights on my small body. Whenever my mom tried to put me into a sitting a position, I immediately slumped and fell over. I had lost all capacity to hold up my body and had to be placed on my back.

"This is not normal," my mom said to one of her sisters. "Something is wrong with Uyen (my Vietnamese name). I have to take her to the hospital right now!"

My mom rushed me to Saigon Children's Hospital—a modern, state-of-the-art facility for its time. There, a doctor used a small rubber hammer to tap my little knees and elbows. Nothing happened. The normal reflexive responses should have been small bounces in my lower arms and legs, but there were none.

"Your daughter has polio," the doctor said. "She's paralyzed from the neck down. She may remain this way for the rest of her life."

Then he handed my mom a small vial of medicine with the German name HOP printed on it. He instructed my mom to give me drops of this liquid, which resembled water, several times a day. The doctor cautioned my mom, "I don't know if this medicine will do anything to help your daughter. Just give it to her until the medicine runs out."

Shocked and devastated, my mom took me home, weeping all the way. When we arrived, one of my aunts, who lived across the street, opened the taxi door for my mom and lifted me out of her arms. My grandmother followed close behind to help my mom out of the taxi and into the house. As soon as she got inside, my mom headed towards the house phone to call my dad at work. Fortunately, he was not deployed to the battlefield at the time and was working close to home.

"Sorry," the secretary told her, "he's in the middle of an important meeting and can't be disturbed."

"This is an emergency!" my mom cried.

When my dad finally came on the phone, my mom barely managed to choke out her words between heavy sobs. "You have to come home right now! Uyen has polio. She is paralyzed from the neck down. The doctor said she may never be able to walk."

My dad rushed home and found me on my back—motionless, silent, and staring vacantly at the ceiling. I usually smiled, made eye contact, squealed with delight, and waved my arms and legs whenever I saw him. Now I showed no signs of even recognizing him. The change was shocking and filled him with dread.

"It was one of the worst days of my life!" my dad told me years later. "I rushed home and thought at first that you were dead. You were lying so still on your back, staring up at the ceiling. When I got closer, I was relieved to see that you did blink. But you didn't recognize me or respond like you usually did. It was heartbreaking and excruciating to see you lying there completely paralyzed and defenseless. I felt so helpless!"

My mom was equally upset. "I thought about how you would not be able to have a normal life," she said, "how you would not be able to walk, play, go to school like other kids, or get married and have your own children. The spark in your eyes, and your happy, playful, and energetic disposition disappeared completely. You were no longer you."

I was one of the many victims of the huge polio epidemic that broke out in South Vietnam at this time. An infectious disease caused by a virus, polio spreads from person to person and attacks the brain and spinal cord, causing paralysis. Overnight, this disease turned me into a quadriplegic.

After the diagnosis, my parents brought me to various specialists, desperate to find out if anything could be done to reverse the paralysis. All the Western-trained doctors gave me a poor prognosis and prepared my parents for the worst. My parents also brought me to see a Chinese medicine doctor, who recommended that my parents massage a specific foul-smelling medicinal oil into my arms and legs three times a day.

Shortly after this appointment, my dad was deployed yet again onto the battlefield. Given that my mom was a single-parent and pregnant with my second sister, she did not have the time or energy to massage me with the medicine as prescribed. Instead, she used large pieces of gauze, soaked them with the medicine, and then bandaged them to my arms and legs. She did this consistently and prayed for the best.

On the evening of January 30th, 1968, the skyline was suddenly illuminated with a reddish orange tint. Multiple loud explosions from bombs shook our house and rattled the pictures on the ancestor altar. Each blast sounded like it was getting closer and closer. The heavy, burnt smell of artillery saturated the air as deafening sounds of heavy gunfire engulfed our once peaceful neighborhood. Fires and debris lined the streets. The Viet Cong were launching a massive attack on Saigon. The entire city was in lockdown mode.

My mom was home alone with us during the attack. She was twenty-two years old, single-parenting me, a fourteen-month-old quadriplegic, and my younger sister Ngan, who was two months old.

My dad was deployed yet again—this time fighting in one of the biggest and bloodiest battles of the Vietnam War, the Tet Offensive. This offensive was launched as a massive surprise attack by the North Vietnamese People's Army of Vietnam, the Viet Cong, on the South Vietnamese Army of the Republic of Vietnam, during the Tet holiday, the Vietnamese new year. The Viet Cong military campaign targeted over a hundred cities. Saigon was one of them.

My mom became the second generation of women in our family to be saddled with the burdens of single-parenting due to war. As the bombs shook our house, traumatic memories of her own escapes years earlier flooded her mind. She paced back and forth, sweating profusely and crying as her heart raced, gripped by intense anxiety. She looked at my sister and me, wondering whether my dad would survive this colossal battle.

Thankfully, my dad did return from this battle in one piece. However, he had almost died when a stray bullet struck the edge of his helmet, rotating it 180 degrees.

In August of the same year, when I was two years old, still paralyzed from the neck down, my sister Ngan became ill. She was feverish, coughing, and had a stuffy nose, which at nine months old interfered with her ability to eat. My mom grew worried and brought Ngan to see the pediatrician.

"The baby has a cold," the doctor told my mother. "She should get better in a few days. Give her aspirin to keep the fever down and suction her nose several times a day right before she takes the bottle."

My mom went home and did as the doctor instructed. But Ngan's condition didn't improve—in fact it grew progressively worse by the hour. By evening, Ngan was struggling to breathe. Her lungs rattled with each breath and she was beginning to turn purple. Frantic, my mom called the doctor, who rushed to our home and examined my sister.

"I must apologize," she said. "I misdiagnosed your daughter. She has pneumonia and is very close to dying."

"Oh my God, how can this be? You told me this morning she had a cold. Now my baby is dying! Oh God! Please don't let this true!"

Thankfully, my maternal grandmother and aunts were there to support my mom through this agonizing incident. Within the hour, Ngan passed away.

My grandfather immediately alerted my dad's platoon to inform him of the terrible news. Within twenty-four hours, he'd come home.

Dressed in his crisply pressed uniform and his flawlessly polished black boots, my dad strode purposefully into the house. His swollen eyes, flushed face, and locked jaw spoke volumes, but he didn't utter a word. He walked over to Ngan's crib, lifted his baby girl out of the crib and held her, as tears streamed down his face. "She looked so perfect, beautiful, and peaceful. I tried to remember everything about her," my father later said, "her smile, her sweetness, her smell, her laugh, the way she used to babble and crawl over to me."

Then he lifted his head to the sky to recite a prayer for his precious daughter, the one who had been taken away from him too soon. He returned Ngan to her crib and went over to my grief-stricken mother who sat on a chair in a corner of the room. My dad held her close as she wept and wailed inconsolably in his arms.

My mom remembers, "My legs felt like wet spaghetti. I couldn't stand or walk. For months, I was haunted by the sights and sounds of that horrible day when Ngan died—the way she struggled to breathe, how her chest heaved up and down and her lungs rattled with each exhale."

Two months after Ngan's death, my sister KimUyen was born. Miraculously, she looked exactly like Ngan.

"I was so thrilled when I saw KimUyen for the first time," mom told me. "She was Ngan's twin! They had the same exact face, duplicate set of dimples, similar folds in their hands, arms, and legs, and the same temperament. I was so thankful that God had mercy on me and brought my baby Ngan back to me in the form of KimUyen. God must have known that this was what I needed in order to move on. It made Ngan's death more bearable."

When I was initially infected by the polio virus and became a quadriplegic, the doctors told my parents that my prognosis was bad, that I would probably never be able to sit upright or walk. As it turned out, they were wrong. By the time I was three years old, I had regained the ability to sit up. Then one day, when I had been sitting quietly in my crib playing with my stuffed animals and baby dolls, my mom suddenly noticed that I was trying to pull myself up to a standing position. Her heart leapt with excitement. My tiny hands were gripping and pulling so tightly on the bars of the crib that my knuckles turned white.

Once I had pulled myself to my knees, I took a brief rest. Then, with great concentration and effort, I grabbed the top rail of the crib with my right hand to pull myself up while simultaneously willing my tiny legs—right first, and then left—into a squatting position. Finally my left hand grabbed onto the top bar, and I stood up for the first time!

"You had a huge smile on your face," my mom said, "and the sparkle in your eyes returned. It was the most amazing thing to see the immense determination in your eyes as you pulled yourself up. I was so happy to see that! It was truly a miracle! I cried and thanked God."

Several months after this incident, I took my first steps.

I didn't learn how severely the polio had affected my early functioning until I was in my forties. My mom revealed this information reluctantly, when I asked her about my medical history in preparation for a post-polio evaluation. I could tell it was painful and difficult for her to discuss this topic—that my getting polio was, and still is to some extent, both traumatic and a source of shame for her.

While it was a shock to learn that I was bedridden for the first three years of my life, she gave me a tremendous gift by telling me the truth. From that day forward I have lived with a deep sense of gratitude for my physical mobility and all the freedoms that come with it. I more fully appreciate basic things, such as the capacity to use my arms, legs, hands, and feet—and the ability to be independent. I feel blessed that I was able to give birth to my daughters and was spared the challenges and complications that would have accompanied living a life with quadriplegia.

While I do live with post-polio syndrome, which causes chronic fatigue, pain, weakness, cold intolerance, and a host of other symptoms, I try to be mindful of the fact that I am incredibly fortunate. An awareness of these ordinary, yet profound, blessings gives me the strength to cope with this chronic illness.

CHAPTER 4

My Ordinary Life

In 1975, my family still lived in Saigon, the capital of South Vietnam. I was eight years old and had three younger sisters: KimUyen, NhaUyen, and ThyUyen, ages six, three, and fifteen months, respectively. During this time, our family was financially well-off. My mom worked as a secretary at the Philco Ford Company (an American company), and my father was a major in the army. Both were successful and content with their jobs. Because of my dad's seniority in rank, he no longer had to fight on the battlefield and was primarily stationed in Saigon. It was customary during this time for our family to take beach vacations or travel to visit my dad's family in Can Tho or Long Xuyen during school holidays.

One weeknight after dinner, my sisters and I were sitting on the cool tiled floor in our living room playing house while the ceiling fan blew lightly on us. We were dressed in short, pastel-colored, cotton jumpers, and were preoccupied with cooking our feast of pretend food. We used miniature pink plastic knives and cutting boards to cut up our faux meats and vegetables. I said to my sisters with a smile on my face, "Watch out, don't cut your fingers—the knives are very sharp!"

Then we boiled and fried the food in tiny flower-adorned pots and pans, making sizzling sounds as we giggled and laughed. Feeling left out, my youngest sister, ThyUyen, waddled over, grabbed the miniature plates and bowls, and threw them on the floor. In response, we yelled at her, "Don't do that! Stop it!"

Our live-in nanny promptly intervened by picking ThyUyen up and taking her away for a bath. KimUyen, NhaUyen, and I were relieved that the disrupter was removed. We happily proceeded to ladle our deliciously prepared fake foods into our little plates and bowls.

Suddenly, we heard my parents run into the room panting. My mom was chasing after my dad as she laughed and squealed with delight. My dad was smiling and running, trying to get away from her. She reached out and grabbed his shorts and then I heard a loud *rrrrrrip*. My mom had just torn the entire left side of my dad's shorts open! She cackled loudly with glee while my dad appeared stunned but amused. He swiftly used his left hand to grab the ripped side of his shorts so they would not fall off and expose his you-know-what.

All this raucous commotion frightened KimUyen and NhaUyen, and they burst out crying. I yelled at my parents, "Mom and dad, stop it! Calm down—you're scaring the kids!"

Then there was complete silence. My dad quickly went upstairs to change his shorts while my mom and I tried to console KimUyen and NhaUyen.

I tried to reassure my sisters by saying, "It's okay, don't cry. Mommy and daddy were just having fun with each other!"

Throughout my childhood in Vietnam, it was common to witness my parents being playful and overtly affectionate with one another. This created a warm, loving, and happy home environment for my sisters and me.

Our home life in Vietnam included many festive holidays, especially Christmas and Tet (Lunar New Year). Every year on the first day of December, my parents took out our artificial Christmas tree, decorated it with colorful, shiny ornaments and silver streamers, and displayed it at the center of a tall table in our living room. To the right of the tree stood an Advent calendar, which had little doors that we would open each night to help us count down the days until Christmas. To the left of the tree was an ornate, fragile ceramic nativity scene that included statues of the Virgin Mary, baby Jesus, Joseph, the three wise men, several sheep, a shepherd boy, and two angels.

Our last Christmas Eve in 1974 began with a big, festive feast. After dinner, my sisters and I quickly got into our pajamas and scampered out to the front porch with our light blankets and pillows for Christmas tales. The temperature was mild and springlike. A half moon hung overhead, and the sky was illuminated with millions of stars. On the porch, we huddled close to our parents, eager to hear them take turns telling us Christmas stories.

My mom went first. Her stories contained a lot of details, action, and suspense, which gripped our attention and sent my siblings and me to the edge of our seats. In between tales, we all looked up into the sky and listened for Santa and his reindeer.

"Oh look, is that Santa over there?" My mom said. "Do you hear the sleigh bells ringing yet? Listen carefully or else you'll miss Santa!"

Then my dad told his Christmas stories, which were more subdued, less descriptive, and lulled us into a state of relaxation. By the time my dad launched into his second story, we were yawning and falling asleep. My parents carried us to our beds and tucked us in.

In the morning, my sisters and I jumped out of our beds and sprinted to the living room. Our eyes lit up with delight as we saw the brightly wrapped presents placed next to our pairs of socks. (In Vietnam, we didn't use Christmas stockings.) Each one of us received one present. We picked up our presents and tore into the packages to see what was inside. I was ecstatic to get my very own miniature cooking set that year!

Tet, the Vietnamese New Year, arrived about a month later. Tet is the most important holiday in Vietnam and usually occurs in January or February, depending on the lunar calendar, in which the months are coordinated with the cycles of the moon. Everyone took at least a week off to enjoy the festivities and visit family and friends. My sisters and I each received a new pair of shoes and a tailor-made red *ao dai,* a traditional Vietnamese dress. We all wore the color red during Tet since it was supposed to bring us good luck throughout the year.

A couple of days before Tet, my mom and our nanny thoroughly cleaned our house since it was considered bad luck to clean within the first week of the new year. It was believed that any cleaning or sweeping would cause good luck and wealth to be swept out of the house. Our ancestor altar was also decorated with beautiful flowers, vivid fruits, and brightly colored incense sticks.

On the morning of Tet, my family and I put on our new outfits and headed off to mass. Then in the afternoon we went to a Buddhist temple. That evening, we gathered with my mom's family to eat a delicious feast filled with specialty dishes such as stewed pork with eggs, noodles, and sticky rice cakes. Afterwards we performed a ceremony to honor our ancestors by lighting incense, praying, and bowing to them. Then the wishing portion of the Tet ritual began. My parents (since they were the oldest) offered my grandparents tea and wished them an auspicious new year. Then my mom's other siblings followed suit, according to their birth order, to wish my grandparents a good year.

My favorite part of the evening culminated with the kids wishing the adults. A typical wish went something like, "I wish you good health, happiness, prosperity, and professional success in this coming year." In return, the adults wished us with sentiments such as, "academic success," "obey your parents," and "be a good child." Then they gave us ornately decorated red packets stuffed with new, crisp bills, called "lucky money." It was always exciting to admire the beautiful designs on the red packets and then look inside to see how much each packet contained.

The best part was totaling up the amount of money we'd been given by the end of the evening. We repeated this wishing ritual throughout the week with all our other relatives and our parents' friends. Because I have a large extended family and my parents had a lot of friends, my siblings and I accumulated a large sum of money by the end of the Tet festival, which allowed us to splurge on whatever our hearts desired.

Me in the first grade (1972), in my school uniform.

Every weekday morning, our chauffeur arrived promptly at seven-thirty. The chauffeur always dropped me and my sister off at school first, and then would take my dad to work. I sat in the back of the car to my dad's right, and KimUyen was to his left. Both KimUyen and I wore our school uniform—a pure white top, navy skirt, and white closed-toe shoes. I was six years old and in the first grade.

Dad in his uniform in 1972.

My dad looked so handsome in his crisply pressed army green uniform adorned with shiny pins and medals of rank and valor. His black lace-up boots were shiny and flawless. He embodied a sense of quiet confidence and solidity. As we were being driven, he would set a stack of papers on his black, rectangular briefcase, read the contents of the pages carefully, and then render his signature on the documents. This was one of the early indications I had that my father had an important job, although I did not know exactly what he did for a living. His professionalism, sturdiness, and humility easily gained him the respect of his subordinates and peers. They often told my mother that he was a kind and effective leader who exhibited both confidence and paternal warmth. These qualities contributed to his swift ascent in rank throughout his military career.

One day at school, my teacher called me up to the front of our second-grade class to recite the history lesson. My heart sank and then accelerated as I tried to walk as slowly as possible towards the front of the classroom. Once there, I faced my classmates—my legs felt wobbly and I broke out in a cold sweat. My mind went completely blank. I couldn't remember a single word from the lesson! I was petrified and humiliated. I opened my mouth and struggled to articulate words, but nothing came out. Awkward silence filled the room. Then my teacher yelled, "Put out your hand! This is what happens when you do not memorize your lesson!"

She hit my hand with a ruler multiple times, each blow burning and stinging my palm.

On that day, I learned a valuable lesson. When your friends tell you that putting the "magic leaf of memorization" into your book will enable you to memorize the lessons without studying, don't believe them. I was foolish enough to trust this tip, and had gone to a specific tree to harvest the leaves and put them in my books.

Luckily, my teacher refrained from hitting me too many times, since my parents had a close relationship with the owner of the school, Father Thinh, who was both a priest and a general in the South Vietnamese army. He was my father's professional and spiritual mentor, and treated my dad like a son. This priest was so kind and playful that whenever he spotted me on the school playground he would come over to give me a big hug, a tickle, and a piece of delicious French or

American chocolate. This made me feel special and contributed significantly to the positive regard in which I held priests.

———∞∞∞———

One weekday afternoon after catechism, I came out of class and didn't see our chauffeur. He usually waited for me right outside the building. I walked to the front gate and stood there for what felt like an eternity. With each passing minute, I grew more impatient. Then I had an idea. *I'm tired of waiting! I'm going to walk home by myself. I can find my way!*

Even though I had never walked home before, I hiked the two miles home, crossing several busy and dangerous highways. Cars, busses, trucks, bicycles, and motorcycles whizzed by me as I strolled steadily towards home. Before each crossing, I carefully looked both ways, as I had been previously instructed by my parents.

The chauffeur was frantic when he arrived at the school thirty minutes late and discovered I was no longer there. He rushed to my house, explained the situation to my mom, and got down on his knees to beg her for forgiveness. My mom alerted my dad to the situation, and he rushed home immediately from work. He made a police report and a search was quickly launched. My parents were beside themselves, imagining the worst—there had been a recent rash of child abductions in Saigon at this time.

Of course, I knew none of this when I reached home. I ambled nonchalantly through the front door and was surprised by all the commotion. My parents let out an audible sigh of relief, while the chauffeur yelled at me with a tremble in his voice, "Oh my God—thank God you are okay! You scared me to death! Don't ever do that again!"

My compassionate parents didn't fire the man. In fact, they consoled and reassured him, seeing how shaken he was by the incident.

Whenever my parents spoke of this event after that, they highlighted their amazement at my "gutsiness," my ability to remember the route home, and the miracle that I did not get run over or kidnapped.

"You were daring like that, and strong-willed—not afraid of anybody or anything."

CHAPTER 5

War Intrudes

One evening early in 1975, my family and I were sitting around talking. Suddenly, loud explosions pierced our ears. Bombs and gunfire shook our house and rattled the pictures on the ancestor altar.

"Get under the bed *now*," my father yelled, "and stay there until I tell you to come out!"

My mom picked up my youngest sister and herded all of us under the bed with her. In the front room, my dad took out his handgun and stood guard at the door. My heart raced wildly, and my body shook as we waited under the bed. Meanwhile, my mom chanted continuously, "Jesus, Maria, Joseph, please protect us. Jesus, Maria, Joseph, please keep us from harm."

Such incidents occurred multiple times during March of 1975. The Viet Cong onslaught from the North was so powerful that it forced a massive retreat of the South Vietnamese forces throughout the highlands, Hue, and Da Nang. At the same time the Viet Cong sent a great number of troops directly into Saigon. This gunfire and bombing that we heard was the beginning of the siege of our city and the final victory for North Vietnam.

During this time in my life, I was surrounded by a large and close-knit extended family. I was very close to my maternal grandparents, aunts, and uncles, who lived across the street from us. My mom's four youngest siblings, who are only two to six years older than me, were like siblings.

In March of 1975, my grandfather, who worked at the American embassy, learned that South Vietnam's demise was imminent, though it was unclear what the exact date would be. Fortunately, my grandfather was appointed to be a part of the planning committee developing the evacuation plan for South Vietnam. His job was to record the experts' verbal formulations and strategies for the escape, and then draw up an evacuation plan. In doing so, he noticed that there were too few evacuation sites available in Saigon for the large number of people who would be trying to leave.

Given their family's previous history with communism in the North, my grandparents were determined to never live under the terrors of such rule again. My grandfather alerted my parents to what he'd learned from the embassy and called a family meeting to devise an escape plan.

He proposed that the family go to Phu Quoc Island, a designated evacuation site about two hundred miles due west of Saigon. The location was ideal, since my mom's maternal uncle was already living there and owned an extra home that he could rent to us. Additionally, the island gave us easy access to boats, the South China Sea, and other Southeast Asian countries. All these conditions maximized our chances of successfully making our escape out of Vietnam once the country fell.

At the family meeting, my grandfather announced that he would take one month off work, without pay, to move the entire family to Phu Quoc.

———— ✺ ————

One late Sunday afternoon in the first week of April, my parents told KimUyen and me they wanted to have a private conversation with us about something. Whatever it was, I knew it was ominous, since my mom's eyes were already puffy and red and my dad looked somber and worried. Once we sat down, my mom wept openly while my dad spoke to us. "We are going on a family vacation to Phu Quoc Island, but I won't be coming with you. You will go with your mom, sisters, grandparents, aunts, and uncles. I must stay here for work. Please tell your friends and teacher you are leaving for a long vacation, but don't tell them any more than that. Do you understand?"

KimUyen and I nodded our heads silently. My heart constricted with worry as I witnessed my parents' unusually grim demeanors. My mom's crying and distress coupled with my dad's tenseness and solemn expression filled me with dread and confusion.

What's going on? I thought. *I've never seen my parents like this before—all sad, tense, and serious. Why is Mom crying, and why does Dad seem so upset if we're going on a vacation? Isn't that supposed to be happy and fun? And why isn't Dad coming with us? We've never gone on a vacation without him!*

Midday on April 6th, my dad took me, my three younger sisters, and my mom to the airport for our flight to Phu Quoc. While waiting there, I sat on my dad's lap, facing him, talking to him about various things. At one point, I playfully and tenderly put the palms of my hands on his cheeks and locked eyes with him while saying, "Daddy, I am going to miss you so much! I can't wait to see you when we get back. Remember, you need to drink a lot of milk to stay strong and healthy."

Suddenly I saw the anguish in my dad's face, and tears streamed from his sad eyes. I had never seen my father cry before. He wrapped his arms tightly around me, cried quietly, and choked out these words: "I'll miss you too. Always remember that I love you!"

Then the loudspeaker announced that it was time to board the plane. My mom told us to get on last, since she wanted more time with my dad. At the final boarding call, my dad hugged and kissed each of his daughters. Then it was my parents' turn to say goodbye. My mom and my dad held onto each other for a very long time and wept in each other's arms.

CHAPTER 6

Heartache in Paradise

My feelings of dread and puzzlement evoked by the somber incidents at the Saigon airport vanished immediately once we arrived on Phu Quoc Island.

A gentle, cool breeze greeted us as we deplaned in the afternoon. Colorful tropical foliage and miles of pristine beaches surrounded us as we drove towards our new temporary home. This spacious new dwelling was located in an attractive, quiet neighborhood; it had an ocean view and was within walking distance of a private beach.

We spent twenty-four days on this paradise island. During our time there, we walked to the secluded beach almost every day and usually had the entire place to ourselves. My sisters and I frolicked in the warm, clear turquoise ocean and built many sandcastles with the fine white sand that tickled and massaged our bare feet. We also played chase for hours on the shoreline as tropical breezes blew through our hair.

Another remarkable aspect of this time was the large sums of money we went through on daily spending sprees. This novel luxury made me feel like I had won the lottery. From my mom's previous escapes and her experiences under communism, she knew that the currency we had would become worthless once the country fell. As a result, she took us out to eat at the very best restaurants and spent lavishly on beauty products and clothes. She also gave me and her siblings the equivalent of $50 or $100 each day to splurge on whatever our hearts desired.

My jaw dropped and my heart leapt with excitement the first time I held one of these large bills between my fingers. I spent most of my money on food, treats, comic books, and going to the movies. We watched Chinese and Indian movies with subtitles, silent Charlie Chaplin films and others from the U.S. like *Love Story,* and movies starring Bridget Bardot and Sophia Loren.

We also liked watching Vietnamese movies. Vietnam had a thriving and profitable film industry, although it was modest by American standards. Vietnam's films were generally well made and created popular stars such as Kieu Chinh, Tham Thuy Hang, and Thanh Nga. Kieu Chinh continued her acting career in America and appeared in the movie *The Joy Luck Club.* Through his connections in Saigon, my father was able to get movies (on reels back then) which we showed in our home, and invited our neighbors to come and watch with us.

On April 24th, my sister NhaUyen, who was three years old at the time, was hanging out at the front of the house with my two youngest uncles and several neighborhood boys. Suddenly, I smelled a strong burning odor and heard a bone-chilling scream that caused the hairs on the back of my neck to stand up.

My youngest uncle Diem yelled, "Oh my God, get help, get help! Her legs are burning!"

My heart constricted as I sprinted outside and saw my sister lying unconscious and limp in my mother's arms, both her legs were charred black.

"I'm taking her to the emergency room!" mom said, weeping. "Please God, please don't let her die!"

Then my mom raced towards the hospital just down the street from our house with my grandparents running after her to provide support.

Several hours later, my grandfather returned home to tell us that NhaUyen had suffered second-degree burns on both of her legs from a gunpowder accident. She would have to remain in the hospital for at least three days. Evidently, the neighborhood boys had been playing with gunpowder and ignited the substance while NhaUyen was standing next to them.

Mom took me to the hospital the following day to visit NhaUyen. Her legs were heavily bandaged, and she moaned continuously from the pain. It was excruciating to see my sister suffer so much. My heart ached for her, but I was powerless to reduce her misery in any substantial way. NhaUyen's screams were particularly agonizing when the nurse came to change her bandages. Nausea and revulsion gripped me as the nurse slowly unrolled my sister's dressings, revealing her inflamed pink flesh and the stench from her raw wounds.

Shortly after he learned of my sister's accident, my dad rushed out to the island on April 25th for an unplanned visit and stayed for two nights. He was visibly worried and distressed when he saw NhaUyen's wounds. My mom pleaded with him not to return to Saigon. But he told her that he could not stay longer and needed to return to his military post.

My dad was a man of honor who would never desert his duties or let his military brothers fight alone, and he remained true to his pledge to defend his country until the bitter end.

CHAPTER 7

Harsh Realities of War

On April 27th, Dad left Phu Quoc Island to return to Saigon. He gave all of us extra-long hugs and waved a tearful goodbye as he departed for his flight home. In my dad's journal, he wrote about how it was for him to say goodbye to us on that day:

> My heart ached as I said goodbye to my family and held them in my arms, wondering if it would be the last time. I felt instinctively that I would not be able to see them again on this island. Within hours after my return to Saigon, all forms of air and ground transportation were halted.

Several hours after he left, I walked into my mom's bedroom and found her crying loudly, her eyes red and puffy. She was cutting out pictures of my dad from an album.

"Mom, what's wrong?" I asked. "Why are you crying? And why are you cutting out pictures of Dad?"

"I'm sorry I have to tell you this harsh truth. Just now, your father has told me that our country is about to be taken over by the communists. They're horrible and ruthless people, and we can't live under them! This is the real reason we came to this island, so we can make a quick escape when Vietnam falls into communist hands. I don't know exactly when this will happen, but it'll probably be very soon. You must promise to keep what I've told you as a secret. If you tell anyone outside of the family about our plan to leave, they'll put us jail. Do you understand?"

"Yes, I understand," I replied. "I'll keep the secret. But why are you cutting out pictures of Dad?"

Mom opened a small bag to show me its contents.

"In here are your dad's two journals, his favorite outfit, and pictures of him. I packed these in case we never see him again. I hope he'll be able to escape when the country falls and reunite with us wherever we end up. But I don't know if that will happen. If he gets captured or killed, we'll only have these things to remember him by."

The next day, as I was in the living room with my sisters, my mom brought each of us a silver dog-tag necklace. She put one on each of my sisters, and then pulled me into her bedroom and shut the door.

"This is your dog tag. It has your name and birthdate in the front, and my and your dad's names and our Saigon home address in the back. Keep it hidden inside your shirt, so no one can see it. We don't want people to suspect that we are planning to leave. During our escape, if you get separated from the rest of the family, you have to go up to a nice adult woman and say, 'I am lost. Here is my address. Please take me home and my parents will pay you.' Can you say that? Practice saying it with me right now."

I repeated these words out loud in front of my mom over and over again until I fully memorized them: "I am lost. Here is my address. Please take me home and my parents will pay you."

Then my mom put the dog tag on me, hiding it under my shirt so it was not visible. It felt cold against my skin, and I hated wearing it because of what it represented: forced separation from my dad as well as fear, danger, and uncertainty. I prayed to God every night that I wouldn't be separated from my family during the escape. I prayed that I would never have to say those absolutely terrifying words to an adult.

———— ∞ ————

After this conversation with my mom, preparations for our escape intensified. Various adult members of our family took turns using binoculars to scan the activities out at sea. The tension in the air was palpable. All the adults were on edge and preoccupied with worry. We no longer went to the beach and were cautioned by my grandfather to stay close to home.

I was assigned a small bag containing one change of clothing, my toothbrush, underwear, and a washcloth. The bag was placed next to my bed, and I was told to grab it immediately whenever the signal was given to leave. My mom warned that we might have to escape in the middle of the night, so I needed to memorize our escape plan and rehearse it until I could execute her orders in my sleep.

As mentioned earlier, Aunt Tuyet was assigned as my escape partner. At night, I slept next to Aunt Tuyet and was cautioned to never leave her side. And most importantly, I had to remember to hold onto her hand during the entire escape.

———— ∞ ————

Late evening on April 29th, while in a deep slumber, I was jolted awake by my grandfather's urgent words, "Get up! Get up! It's time to go! Don't turn on the lights!"

What followed were the two hasty and frightening flights to sea described at the beginning of the book.

CHAPTER 8

Journey at Sea

Having been rescued by a kind stranger and carried from the scow to the ship, I found myself alone, surrounded by the vast expanse of the South China Sea.

After a long while, the thunderous cries from those around me subsided, and I rose gingerly to my feet. Numbness and exhaustion weighed me down as I struggled to walk. By now, the ship was lit by a few dim lights, revealing a massive wall-to-wall layering of people on the top and bottom decks. From the top deck peering down, the people on the bottom tier resembled a massive colony of ants tightly packed together. This sight overwhelmed and repelled me, so I chose to remain on the top deck. I wandered around the ship for several hours, looking for my family. With each passing minute, I grew more despondent and afraid. The image of KimUyen being left behind on the fishing boat with my grandparents and aunts replayed relentlessly in my head. It took me to a dark place.

What if my whole family is still back there and I'm on this ship by myself? What if the communists captured and killed them? Oh my God, what would become of me! How am I supposed to survive? And where is this ship taking me?

Warm tears flooded my eyes and a lump lodged in my throat as I continued searching for my family.

It was late into the night when I finally reunited with my mom, sisters NhaUyen and ThyUyen, and two aunts and two uncles. I learned that after I had jumped onto the scow, my mom had put one of her legs into the packed scow to create a small space. Then she jumped on, holding ThyUyen and NhaUyen. "Help me—please help me and my babies!" she cried as she writhed and squeezed her way towards the front of the scow. Finally she and my sisters were lifted up from the scow onto the ship by the navy officers.

My mom and I first spotted each other from afar on the top deck. She walked mechanically towards me with a blank, distant look on her face that was void of any emotion. She was the zombie version of my mom. There was no smile, embrace, or squeals of delight when we reunited. She just took my hand and lead me to a small space where the others sat, equally dazed and expressionless.

We were on the ship for four nights and five days. After the first day, my mom seemed more like her old self again. She made eye contact when she spoke with me, and her emotions returned. But that was the only faint bright spot. Conditions on the ship were appalling. Overcrowding was a huge problem. The eight of us crammed into a space the size of a large kitchen table. We sat with our legs folded up to our chest and took turns stretching them out. We also slept in shifts, since there was only space for a few of us to lie down at a time. There were no partitions; all the passengers were packed in like sardines.

Due to the unsanitary and very cramped conditions, a rampant outbreak of pinkeye occurred. Our eyes became red, painful, and oozed with an unpleasant discharge. There was no medical care to treat them. Nor was there much in the way of food and water. At one point, we were given canned foods—but no can opener. Then we were offered porridge—not an appetizing option, given that it was cooked in huge garbage cans in the open air, next to the bathrooms.

I ate and drank very little during this voyage, just nibbled on a few crackers spread with peanut butter and took small sips of water. The entire experience made me nauseous and lethargic.

My fifteen-month-old sister, ThyUyen had no milk and was slowly starving to death. KimUyen had the formula in her escape bag, but she was left behind on a fishing boat with my maternal grandparents. ThyUyen constantly puckered her lips while crying and moaning the word "milk" over and over again. Two days into the voyage, she became weaker and her cries grew more faint. She was slowly slipping away from us. Frantic, my mom went around the ship, begging other passengers for milk to feed her baby girl. Several times, my mom got down on her knees, sobbing and pleading, "Please, anyone, please have mercy. If any of you have milk, please give her some. She'll die without milk."

Eventually one woman offered some of her baby's formula to my sister. We wept with gratitude for this woman's generosity. She shared the little milk she had, even though her own child also needed it. It saved my sister's life.

Meanwhile, NhaUyen, in constant pain from her severely burned legs, cried or moaned continuously. Her bandaged legs oozed an incessant pungent discharge, and she had great difficulty moving and walking. Since no medical care was available to treat her raw and inflamed legs, she could only endure the misery, while we watched helplessly.

Other distressing events were going on all around us. People frequently argued, yelled, and screamed at one another. Accusations of theft of various items were common, and sometimes resulted in physical scuffles. The environment onboard the ship was chaotic and frightening—an aura of survival of the fittest set in.

One of the worst experiences on the ship for me was the daily trip to the toilet. It was located on the upper deck and consisted of a tiny wooden stall exposed to the elements, where I had to straddle and squat to do the deed. Between my legs was a huge gap open directly to the ocean below. Each time I went, my heart raced—the ferocious winds seemed to blow right through me, making it difficult to maintain my balance and footing. I knew I could fall through the opening and no one would know how I had disappeared. As I held onto the sides of the stall for dear life, I wondered how many kids had already fallen to their deaths. I avoided using the toilet as much as possible.

On the ship we encountered some neighbors from Saigon. They told us they had seen communist soldiers enter our home while my dad was inside and heard gunfire. They felt almost certain that my dad had been killed.

Hearing this news sent me into deep despair. I had no appetite, wept a lot, and became apathetic as overwhelming feelings of sadness and emptiness consumed me. My mom, however, carried on courageously, expressing words of encouragement and hope. She reminded us to be thankful that we all made it onto the ship. "Even if we never see your dad, KimUyen, or the rest of our family again," she said, "we must stay strong, move ahead, and make a new future for ourselves."

But at night, my mom cried softly to herself, thinking I couldn't hear her. I realized that my brave, strong, courageous mom was also frightened and sad. I wondered whether we would all survive this journey at sea. And I wondered where the ship was taking us.

On the fifth night, we arrived on the island of Guam, a U.S. territory.

While fleeing Vietnam and living through the horrendous conditions on the ship have been two of the most difficult experiences of my life, they have also provided me with many gifts. I feel very grateful that my family and I have survived three generations of war. My mom's family's history of escape has shown me that I come from a legacy of strong and resilient people. This awareness has kept me grounded and provided me with hope and encouragement as I have waded through some of life's rough waters.

I'm also grateful that, because we survived the dangerous journey out of Vietnam, my family and I have had the opportunity to live in one of the greatest democratic countries in the world. This realization fuels my fervent desire to help other immigrants and refugees who flee their countries in search of a better life here in America. And having lived through conditions of semistarvation makes me appreciate the daily blessings of having my basic needs met. I now have food, clothing, and shelter—every day. It's something I try to be mindful of and not take for granted.

Over the years, I've also reflected on the kindness of the man who scooped me up in his arms and carried me up onto the ship, as well as the selflessness of the woman who gave ThyUyen milk when she was starving on the ship. It's amazing to think about these people's generosity, compassion, and humanity, given the dangerous and dire conditions.

The gift of this adversity is realizing that, even in the darkest and most desperate of times, there are good people who care and want to help. This comforting thought gives me great hope in humanity. It also reminds me to reach out for help during challenging times, even when my inclination may be to isolate. In turn, I make every effort to help others who are in need whenever possible.

The escape also anchors my worldview, personality, and life's choices. For example, even though I can be as much of a complainer as the next person, my inclination tends towards optimism, viewing the world through the lens of gratitude, and feeling hopeful and positive about life and our human race. The memories of the escape ground me with the perspective that most things are solvable and manageable, if we are willing to work at it, since most of life's challenges are not life or death.

I also attribute my choice to become a clinical psychologist to my escape experience. Going through my own adversity planted deeply a seed of desire to help others and the conviction that true happiness comes from our ability to decrease the suffering of our brothers and sisters. It inspires me to be an instrument of hope and healing for others in whatever way possible.

I believe that people are generally capable, resilient, and have a desire to move towards growth, even in the face of challenging life circumstances. These assumptions make me optimistic about the human capacity to heal from traumas and contribute to my belief that most of us can overcome hardships, if we are able to access adequate help and support. These beliefs enable me to remain hopeful, steady, and tenacious in my work with clients. I'm constantly in awe of how survivors of trauma manage to survive and thrive under the most difficult of circumstances. My personal experience informs this worldview, as have the experiences of numerous clients I've had the privilege of working with through the years.

CHAPTER 9

Reunion

On the evening of May 5th, 1975, we arrived on Guam—and at Tent City. The weather was oppressively hot and humid, causing our skin to feel sticky and our clothes to cling to our bodies. The roads were covered with dead toads flattened by various vehicles. A bus drove us to the processing center. Then we were directed to our assigned army-green cloth tent. Inside was a dirt floor and wooden cots covered with a coarse canvas material. Fortunately, we had a tent all to ourselves, so we didn't have to share with strangers.

The camp had ten sections, each with its own mess hall. There were lines everywhere, for everything: the mess hall, portable toilet stalls, showers.

Basic activities of daily living, such as showering, were humiliating and dehumanizing. The shower consisted of a large cloth tent with a huge open space inside, a concrete floor, and a large drain in the middle. There were no partitions for privacy. Shower spouts with low water pressure protruded from metal pipes overhead. The women in the camp often complained that the American military police, who were supposed to keep them safe by guarding the tent, often peeked in on them while they showered. Every time I was there, I overheard women warning each other about the Peeping Toms. Hearing this made me feel wary and unsafe. The complaints fell on deaf ears, and no changes for our safety, privacy, and dignity were ever made.

Three times a day, we had to stand in long lines at the mess hall while the scorching sun beat down on us, as we waited to get our meals. The worst was lunch, since it was during the hottest part of the day. Despite that, it was interesting and exciting that first week to anticipate what foods awaited us at the front of the line. I enjoyed tasting the various American dishes that I had never tried before.

Breakfast was the best meal, usually consisting of orange juice, scrambled eggs and toast, porridge, pancakes, biscuits with gravy, or cereal, and lots of milk. I guessed the meal planners didn't know that many Vietnamese are lactose intolerant. Many people developed severe, painful gastrointestinal reactions to the milk.

Lunch usually consisted of sandwiches or soup. Dinner was so unremarkable that I can't even remember what we had other than fried chicken. After the initial week, the menu repeated itself, quickly becoming monotonous. By our fourth week in the camp, I had memorized it.

———— ⚭ ————

Loudspeakers surrounded Tent City, making continuous announcements from morning till night of people's names and tent addresses (section and number). This was one of the ways family members had of locating each other. The other was to wait at the various bus stops that brought in the latest arrivals.

I went to these bus stops daily with my mom or aunts to look for family members. We lacked hats or umbrellas to shield us from the harsh sun, which burned our skin, and the heat and humidity made it painful and frustrating to stand outdoors for long periods of time, especially when our efforts always resulted in failure. I dreaded these daily trips.

Throughout this period, my mom remained strong, positive, and efficient. She took care of our daily needs at the camp, including getting meals and caring for my younger sisters and me, as well as her siblings. She tried to reassure us that everything would be all right and we would be reunited with our loved ones soon. Every evening, we said the rosary as a family and prayed for the safety and reunification of our family. But late at night, I heard my mom weeping softly, when she thought we were asleep and couldn't hear her. Hearing her cry concerned and alarmed me. It made me realize that she was not as strong as she appeared during the day.

After failing to find my father and any other members of our family day after day, I became discouraged. I wondered whether my dad was indeed dead, as our neighbors had reported, or if he was in prison being tortured by the communists. I also missed my sister KimUyen terribly, and felt sad whenever I thought of the possibility of never seeing her again.

Four days after coming to Guam, I was at the tent with an aunt. I'd chosen not to accompany my mom, NhaUyen, and my ten-year-old uncle Diem to the mess hall to get lunch because the weather was so hot. Shortly after they left, uncle Diem ran back to the tent, yelling over and over, "Your dad is here! Your dad is here!"

Hearing this made me really angry with uncle Diem. I thought that he was playing another practical joke on me, as he had done many times before. Tears streamed down my face as I ran after him and began hitting him and yelling at him.

"You are a bad and mean person for joking like that! It's not funny!"

But within ten minutes, my dad came walking towards our tent with my mom and NhaUyen. My dad made it to Guam! This was not a dream. It was really my dad walking towards me, picking me up, and giving me a big hug. In his arms, I felt safe and secure again for the first time in months.

While my mom stood in line at the mess hall with NhaUyen and uncle Diem, she felt someone tap her on the shoulder, from the back.

She turned around, and it was my dad there facing her, in the flesh. He had actually arrived at Tent City one day ahead of us. He'd initially gone to the various bus depots every day to look for us, but then quickly abandoned the plan, deciding it was inefficient and unlikely to be fruitful. Instead, he devised a new strategy: going to one mess hall each day. He spent the entire day at each location, keeping watch throughout breakfast, lunch, and dinner, observing every person who passed through the line. He arrived daily before the first person was served breakfast, and left only after the last person was served dinner. Given the fact that we all needed to eat, he was confident that one of us would eventually appear in one of the lines. Since there were ten mess halls, he was hopeful that we would be reunited within ten days.

His strategy worked. He found my mom on the third day of his search. My dad said that it was very fortunate that NhaUyen and uncle Diem had accompanied my mom to the mess hall on that day, because he would not have recognized my mom had she gone by herself. She had lost about fifteen pounds since they'd seen each other, and her skin had burned to a deep brown from the daily exposure to the sun during her own searches for him.

My mom said the same thing about my dad—that she wouldn't have spotted him if he hadn't come up to her, since his complexion was similarly darkened from the days of keeping watch at the mess hall in his daily searches for her. My mom wept loudly in the middle of the mess hall line, as my dad held her in his arms again.

That evening, we prayed to thank God for reuniting us and petitioned the Divine to bring us back together with the rest of the family. This reunification with my dad was one of the happiest moments of my life!

When my dad had returned from visiting us on Phu Quoc Island, he said, people in Saigon seemed anxious and antsy. On the day he returned, April 27th, he decided not to sleep at home anymore, because he felt there was a higher likelihood of being captured there once the country fell. He had gotten word that the South Vietnamese troops were being ordered to retreat at an alarming rate.

My dad returned to his post and worked with his colleagues to secure their location. They were working rotating two-day shifts to guard the post. On the evening of the 29th, he changed into his civilian clothes after his shift ended and immediately went to my elementary school to see his mentor, Father Thinh. Father Thinh urged my dad to stay at the school for the evening, since it was less likely to be bombed or attacked. He also handed my dad ten packets of instant noodles, so he would have food in case of an emergency. My dad stayed at the school that night but was unable to sleep. He was preoccupied by his concerns about us, gripped by foreboding that the country's demise was imminent, and worried that he might not be able to escape. The constant racket of helicopters airlifting people out of the country from the rooftop of the American embassy did not help.

"They had helicopters going nonstop, picking people up from the roof of their embassy," he told us. "The helicopters signaled to me that the end was near. I thought about all of you and wondered how you all were doing. Mostly, I worried about your safety and whether the family would be able to escape. I was also anxious for daylight to come, so I could execute my own exit plan."

By six o'clock in the morning on the 30th, the roar of the helicopters had ceased, only to be replaced by the loud sounds of cars and mopeds rushing through the city. My dad dressed quickly and left the school. Wearing his uniform would have made him a target for capture, imprisonment, and torture once Vietnam fell into communist hands, so he was grateful for his civilian clothes. He carried only a small bag, which contained one change of clothing, the dry noodles Father Thinh had given him, and a few essential toiletries. On the street, the chaotic, frenetic energy of the city, driven by people's fear, was palpable.

"As chaos and anxiety enveloped our city like I had never seen before," he said, "the people's worried and frantic faces signaled terror and pandemonium! They rushed about with a sense of urgency. It was clear that the demise of the country was approaching any minute."

My dad had headed to the American embassy first, and was alarmed by what he witnessed there. The doors were wide open, and looters were running in and back out with various items they had stolen: typewriters, chairs, desks. On the rooftop, one silent helicopter sat, surrounded by armed American soldiers. My dad was pessimistic about being able to leave the country by air—all flights in and out of the country seemed to be grounded, and most of the embassy employees had already been airlifted out. So he went to the pier, hoping to escape by boat.

By then he was extremely worried and grew increasingly pessimistic about his chances of escaping. He thought that at any moment he could be captured by the Viet Cong. Once there, he jumped on a boat loaded with people, but it had no captain. He then got off the boat and began walking to the opposite side of the pier, joining a man in uniform who was also searching for transport. Suddenly, they noticed a small Vietnamese Navy boat moving speedily towards them.

"I need a machinist," the captain shouted as he drew close. "Are either of you machinists?"

The man standing next to my dad yelled, "Yes, I am a machinist!"

This fellow pointed to the label on his uniform, which indicated that he was an engineer in the navy. The boat slowed, pulled close to the pier, and the captain gestured to my father and the engineer to jump onboard. It never came to a full stop and as soon as they had jumped aboard it accelerated and darted off.

"The minute I jumped onto the ship," my dad told us, "I got down on my knees, looked up to the sky, and thanked God and the Virgin Mary for saving my life."

At ten o'clock that morning, my dad heard a radio announcement ordering all South Vietnamese soldiers to drop their weapons and surrender to the communist troops.

"I felt a profound grief at the realization that the communists had defeated us, after all the years of fighting and the countless lives lost. I cried for myself and all my brothers who gave our blood and sweat—and our entire lives—to fight in this war. It was all for naught!"

He told me that this was one of the most painful and demoralizing moments of his life. After devoting his entire life to fighting the war, he came to realize that the war was absolutely senseless. He felt a deep sense of anger and betrayal towards the American government, which he believed had abandoned the South Vietnamese. He was convinced that South Vietnam was more than capable of winning the war "had the American government not deserted us, and if the American military showed a willingness to collaborate with the South Vietnamese troops." At the same time, he never blamed the American soldiers. He felt that the American government had let them down, too. In fact, my dad had a lot of compassion for and felt strongly allied with American Vietnam War veterans. He believed that all American and South Vietnamese soldiers were innocent victims of their misguided governments.

The Vietnamese Navy vessel my father boarded had about three hundred passengers. The boat traveled out to sea for two days and was then met by a large American Navy ship, which would escort it the rest of the way. My dad's English came in handy at that point. He spoke with an American officer onboard and learned that the ship was heading to the Philippines. Once he arrived there, my dad learned that refugees from Phu Quoc Island were being transported to Guam. He immediately boarded a flight to Guam, where he reunited with us.

The joy of our reunion with my dad was dampened by our inability to find KimUyen and the rest of my mom's family. We later learned from my aunts who were with KimUyen that, after the American ship deserted them on the evening of April 30th, their small boat had continued out to sea. At one point, the boat's engine broke down and the vessel took on water due to the forceful winds and current. The crewmen scrambled to bail out the water, while most of the passengers panicked. Eventually the engine got repaired, and the boat returned to shore. Many people got off, but my maternal grandfather insisted that his family stay onboard. He said, "We will die either way. Better to die trying to escape. Stay put on the boat!"

They stayed on the boat until about five the next morning, at which point, they were sprayed with gunfire by communist soldiers. The captain hurriedly took the boat out to sea, and they were rescued by a Vietnamese Navy ship shortly thereafter, which transported them to the Philippines. Serendipitously, one of the officers on the ship that rescued them was our next-door neighbor. He took our family members to his cabin and gave them the VIP treatment, so they had enough to eat and enjoyed a safe and uneventful journey to the Philippines. From there, KimUyen and the rest of the family boarded an American ship, which took them to Guam.

On May 15th, I went to a bus station on Guam with my parents. As several busses parked and groups of passengers disembarked, my parents waded through the crowds, repeatedly yelling out my maternal grandfather's name: "Are Mr. Hinh Sy Ho and his family on this bus?"

Many busses arrived during the next hour, until finally a male passenger responded in a loud booming voice, "Yes, yes! Mr. Ho and his family are on this bus!"

Then I spotted KimUyen slowly making her way towards the front of the bus with my grandparents and aunts. The moment she stepped off the bus, I grabbed and embraced my sister, holding onto her tightly. I didn't want to let go.

The joy I felt at that moment is indescribable. Our family was whole again! It was like they had all returned from the dead.

This experience of losing my family, temporarily, and then reuniting with them, taught me to never take my loved ones for granted. This gift of adversity, learned from the pain of separation caused by war and escape, is forever seared in my mind.

CHAPTER 10

From Guam to Camp Pendleton

On June 4th, 1975, while still on Guam, I received the Catholic sacrament of Confirmation and KimUyen received her first Communion. I was eight years old, and KimUyen was six. Religion and its various rituals continued to play an important part in our lives, even within the confines of a refugee camp and in a foreign land. My maternal grandfather talked with me the day before the mass about the significance of receiving the sacrament of Confirmation. He explained that it symbolized my becoming an adult in the Catholic Church and meant that I was responsible for making my own decisions in my relationship with God and the Church. I was touched and surprised by the tenderness he displayed when we had this conversation.

My maternal grandfather was a brilliant and complicated man, a self-taught structural engineer who was fluent in Vietnamese, French, and English. He read the encyclopedia cover to cover for fun and seemed to know everything under the sun. As a result, every conversation with him was informative and intellectually stimulating. He was a wonderful conversationalist who had a charming and magnetic personality.

He was also very passionate about learning. He valued education so much that when I was in the eighth grade he gave me a set of the Encyclopedia Britannica—a reward prompted by his finding out that I had maintained straight A's for many years and had recently been elected the student body president of my junior high school. I vividly remember the day he took me and my mom to the Britannica sales office to put in the order. He expressed his pride in me—as well as his expectation that I continue to excel in my studies. He reminded me that my accomplishments represented not only my own success but also "the face of our people and country."

No pressure!

My mom and I were shocked when we found out the enormous cost of the purchase. My family's income was under the poverty level at the time, and we barely had enough money to pay our monthly expenses.

As charming and fascinating as my grandfather was, I had always been somewhat fearful of him. He was extremely fierce and strict, while also being intellectually brilliant, artistic, and musical. I wondered whether his work with the French, specifically when he was assigned to the interrogation unit, had affected his personality. It's also possible that he was captured and tortured at some point during the war. Regardless, his sternness and the authoritarian way in which he interacted with me, my mom, grandmother, aunts, and uncles left me feeling afraid of him most of the time. I saw him beating my aunts and younger uncles many times. And once, when I was about seven, I was the recipient of one of his beatings. He had told me more than once not sit on his coffee table. But as children will, at one point I forgot. He pulled me onto the bed and hit me on my bottom with a bamboo rod. The red lines on my behind were there for over a week.

My mom recalls seeing these marks. When I asked her how she responded when she saw them, she replied, "There was nothing I could do. He was my father and could do whatever he wants. As a grown woman, if my father wanted to hit me, I would have to submit. This is part of our cultural belief system and values—the male patriarch has all the power and can do whatever he wants. Our culture is also more accepting of parents hitting their children and views physical punishment as part of good parenting. There is a Vietnamese adage that says, 'If you love your children, give them the rod. If you don't love them, give them sweetness and kindness.'"

———— ∞∞∞ ————

On a late evening in mid-June, my family and I arrived at Camp Pendleton in San Diego, California. During our time on Guam, my dad worked as a volunteer translator to help facilitate the resettlement process for the refugees. This enabled him to talk to some American co-workers there, and from them he learned that California was the most ethnically diverse of the resettlement locations and had the most temperate weather. He discussed these findings with my mom and her family, and it was decided that we would request a move to California. So sometime in mid-June, we boarded a huge Pan Am airplane, and endured the very long flight to San Diego.

Getting out of the plane we were hit with bone-chillingly cold weather. I had never experienced that kind of cold before! While we awaited processing, our teeth chattered, our lips turned purple, and we shivered in our summer outfits, which were appropriate for the hot, humid climate of Guam but not for the frigid nights of San Diego. Our welcome into the camp included receiving a puffy plastic coat, a pair of tennis shoes, blankets, and toiletries. Then we were assigned to a large cloth tent, which we shared with at least four other families, separated from them only by pinned-up bedsheets.

Our beds were wooden cots covered by a thick canvas material and topped with air mattresses. The ground was covered in loose dirt, which usually caked our shoes, feet, and clothing. On windy days, our skin felt like sandpaper, and our hair and scalp became grainy from the dirt blowing all around us. The weather was very hot during the day but cold at night. To cope with the frigid nights, we went to the garbage cans at the mess hall to collect plastic milk bottles, and then filled them nightly with hot water. We put these hot water bottles in our beds at night to keep us warm.

The bathroom facility consisted of rows of portable toilets lined up outside the tents, each with a nauseating stench that's forever engraved in my olfactory memory. The shower facilities were similar to those in Guam—huge open cloth tents with concrete floors and no dividers or shower curtains for privacy. Here again, the process of showering felt unsafe and dehumanizing. The military police continually peeked at the women as they showered. Some of the ladies got so fed up that they went out to confront the Peeping Toms, yelling at them to go away. But nothing was ever done to protect our privacy or stop the humiliation of being treated like objects.

The arrangement of the camp, where four to five families were placed under one tent, put me directly in harm's way. There was a man in his thirties whose cot was next to our family's area, separated only by a hanging sheet. One afternoon, he pulled me to his side of the curtain and showed me a picture of a woman giving a man oral sex.

"You do the same thing to me," he said.

I rejected his command and ran away. He did this another time, and I responded more forcefully, saying no and that I would tell my parents if he ever approached me again. Thankfully, he never pursued me again and left the camp shortly after the second incident.

During our time in Camp Pendleton, my dad worked for the American Red Cross in the children's unit. He was paid $2.15 per hour and given a bicycle. His job was to ride his bike throughout the camp and track down unaccompanied minors (children under the age of eighteen). Then he connected these kids to the Red Cross, who arranged for them to be put into foster care or adopted by American parents. My dad's job enabled him to shop at the PX—the military store—and gave him access to American colleagues who lived outside the camp. As a result, we were able to get some stuff loved by all the kids such as chewing gum.

One day my dad came home from work and surprised us with packages of instant Asian noodles. It felt like Christmas in the camp! The noodles were a welcome change from the bland cafeteria food we had been eating day after day. My first bowl of instant noodles in the camp was an amazing experience. My taste buds exploded with so many delightful flavors! I had a similar episode several weeks after, when one of our tentmates brought home a toaster. All of us kids in the tent were so excited by this novel gadget. We toasted countless slices of bread, stuffing them continuously into our mouths for several hours. We only stopped eating once we and our aching stomachs fell into a toast coma.

On another day, my dad came home with rolls of colorful yarn. My mom was concerned that we were getting bored in the camp, given that we didn't have school or any scheduled kids' activities. She'd asked my dad to purchase the yarn, and she used it to teach me and KimUyen how to crochet hats and scarves. These projects gave us precious time with my mom, allowed the time to pass by more quickly, and created a sense of normalcy within the confines of the camp. Once September and October rolled around, the nights became even colder, and our newly knitted hats and scarves came in handy.

———⊶∞⊷———

Without any acknowledgement or celebration, KimUyen and I turned seven and nine years old, respectively, in Camp Pendleton.

Our family ended up spending almost six months there because we had difficulty finding a sponsor who could accommodate our large group of seventeen people. In mid-October we got word that a Christian church in Northern California had offered to sponsor our family. In preparation for our new life, my dad decided that we should all be given American names.

"If they," he said, meaning Americans, "can't say your name, they won't see you as a person."

He was totally right. His decision reflected his wisdom and the realities that awaited us in the U.S. He knew that most Americans in 1975 had little to no prior contact with Vietnamese people and would feel uncomfortable saying our names. He hoped that having American names would increase our chances of being accepted and decrease the risk of us being marginalized. At the time, the Vietnam War was still a painful reminder for many Americans, the first war their country had ever lost. And American society was still reeling from the effects of the anti-war movement, which was a deep source of contention for a lot of people.

So overnight, each member of our family was given an American name. I was known as GiaoUyen to my family, but Carolee to Americans. My sisters KimUyen, NhaUyen, and ThyUyen, became Betty, Jane, and Kathy, respectively. And my parents were known as Tom and Mary Tran.

On Friday, October 24th, we boarded a short flight, and headed for Lafayette, California. It was strange, exciting, and liberating to leave the confines of the camp, after six months of being separated from the outside world. Finally, we would be free to explore and live in this great country called America!

CHAPTER 11

Humble Beginnings

Our flight landed in Oakland on a clear, crisp, sunny afternoon. A small group of parishioners from the Christian church that sponsored us came to the airport to welcome us. Our group consisted of my maternal grandparents, four aunts, three uncles, my parents, myself and my three younger sisters, and two adoptive "uncles." These two men, in their early twenties, had met my parents in Camp Pendleton and requested to be informally adopted into our family. The drive from Oakland to Lafayette took about twenty minutes. I was struck by the vastness of the roads and how everything looked so open, clean, and expansive.

Once we exited the freeway, lush old trees and emerald green pastures surrounded us as our car steadily climbed the winding narrow road up to the house. All the homes along the road were built on huge, well-manicured plots of land. This initial exposure to our new world was magical and inviting—a huge contrast from the dusty, stark, barren confines of the refugee camps where we had resided for the past six months. The fall air was fresh and crisp—all my senses sparked with excitement and anticipation.

Our first stop was to the house where my maternal grandparents and their younger children would reside—a home owned by a physician and his family who attended the church that sponsored us. They allowed my mom's family to stay in their guest house. After dropping them off, we drove a couple of miles down the road to our new residence, which sat on a hill, nestled between gorgeous mature trees. Our sponsors were another physician and his wife (Dr. and Mrs. O), who also attended the church. Their main residence was located at the front of the lot, while ours was nestled in the back.

Our new beige-colored home was a one-bedroom, one-bathroom in-law cottage; it would house the eight of us: my parents, my sisters and me, and the two adoptive uncles. I was delighted and awed that this new home contained so many rooms—living room, kitchen, bathroom, and bedroom. The change from sharing one large space with multiple families felt extravagant and exciting. The carpeted floor in all the rooms (except for the kitchen), felt luxurious and inviting in contrast to the filthy, dusty ground in the refugee camps. Our new home felt plush, comfortable, and welcoming.

Given that there was only one bedroom, the sleeping arrangements were that my entire family of six occupied the bedroom. My parents had the queen-size bed. Kathy was in a crib next to the bed, and Betty, Jane, and I slept in sleeping bags on the floor. Our adoptive uncles slept in the living room on the sofa bed, which was promptly closed up each morning upon waking.

A week after our arrival, we were relaxing on the sofa after dinner when we heard a loud knock on the front door. My dad went to open the door while I followed closely behind him. I was shocked and terrified to see a group of people staring at us, all dressed in scary-looking costumes and masks. My heart raced and my legs wobbled as I heard them say in unison, "Trick or treat!"

Not understanding what "trick or treat" meant, my dad asked impatiently, "What do you want?"

"Candy," they replied.

My mom ran into the kitchen, grabbed the only bag of Hershey's miniatures chocolate candy we'd had, and gave them the whole thing. We were so shaken by the incident that we quickly shut the door, turned off all the lights, and went to bed early.

Before I fell asleep, I overheard my dad wondering aloud to my mom, "Robbers in America want candy? How odd."

This was October 31st, 1975, our first Halloween in America. It was one of our first experiences of culture shock. Many others were to follow.

———— ✿ ————

The Monday after Halloween, my dad started a job at an auto salvage company, which paid $2.50 per hour. The owner of the company was a member of the same Christian church that our hosts belonged to. My dad was thirty-five years old at the time, and the job was a huge step down for him. He went from being a major in the Vietnamese Army to working as a janitor. But he never complained about this change in his employment status. He was proud of his ability to make an honest living and grateful for the opportunity to support his family financially.

Due to his strong work ethic, within a few years my dad was promoted into a manager position in one of the company's major departments. In this position, my dad's co-manager was a Caucasian American named Lew, who was also a Vietnam War veteran. They worked alongside one another day after day and became fast friends, referring to themselves as "work brothers."

My dad endured many incidents of racial hatred at work. He told us about many aggressive male customers who called him "gook," "chink," and "commy" (short for communist) and screamed demeaning things at him. "Go home Chinaman—you don't belong here!"

they'd shout. "Get out of my country, you gook! Go back to where you came from!"

Several times, customers even spat on him.

I felt protective of my dad and was heartbroken that he had to withstand such humiliation and hostility, but he tried to reassure me. "Nobody can hurt me with their ignorant and hateful words and actions. Their behaviors say more about who they are than who I am. I know who I am—a good Catholic who is devoted to my family, and a soldier who bled and fought for his country until the very end. Nothing anybody says or does will ever change that."

Lew came over to our house for dinner many times and told us about other incidents of racism he witnessed towards my dad. They joked around a lot, and sometimes even laughed at the absurdity of the various hate incidents my dad endured. I was grateful to hear Lew express his outrage towards the perpetrators and share the various ways they skillfully maneuvered these skirmishes at work to protect my dad from harm. It's heartwarming and moving to think of how these two brave veterans, both of whom survived the war on the battlefield, were fighting the battles of racism in America together. They had a deep friendship grounded in mutual caring, admiration, and respect for one other.

Whenever my dad recounted these episodes, he used them to teach my siblings and me about the importance of treating everyone with kindness and respect, regardless of the color of their skin, their religion, their occupation, or their socioeconomic status. He emphasized the importance of hard work and making an honest living to support one's family.

Within several weeks of our arrival, my dad got his driver's license. He was used to driving cars from his time in the military and adapted seamlessly to driving in America. My parents had saved up some money from my dad's job in Camp Pendleton, which enabled them to put down a partial payment for their first used car in America, a red 1972 Toyota Corolla. We were all so excited about this first large purchase. My dad took all of us out for a drive the evening after it was purchased. The price of gas at the time was thirty-five cents a gallon. Having the car allowed our family to be independent from others for transportation and enabled my parents to feel like they were taking baby steps towards attaining the American dream.

My mom was five months pregnant when we arrived in Lafayette. My brother, Robbie, was born in the spring of 1976. We were all elated to have a baby brother in our family of four girls.

My mom started working shortly after Robbie was born. She began by cooking and cleaning for wealthy homeowners in the area. Sometimes she worked two or three jobs to supplement my dad's income. Several of her employers took advantage of her. They paid her less than the minimum wage while requiring her to work twelve-hour shifts and only paying her for eight hours' work. Even though my mom knew her employers were cheating her, she never complained. She swallowed her pride and persevered every single day to do a good job.

"I knew it was not right what my employers were doing, taking advantage of me. But I had no choice; I had to do what was necessary to put food on the table and pay the bills. I never quit a job until I had another one lined up. I know my experience wasn't unusual. There are many immigrants and refugees who are mistreated by their employers."

My mom went on to work as a nurse's aide, a cook, and then as a housekeeper for many years. During school vacations, my siblings and I always went along to help my mom at her housekeeping jobs so that she could have a short respite from her grueling work schedule. The years of hard manual labor took its toll on her body, causing severe chronic pain in her hands, arms, shoulders, and knees.

As a nine-year-old, I was given the responsibility of caring for my four younger siblings after school and on the weekends so my parents could go to work. "We're a team," they said. "We all must work together to make our life in America successful. We go to work while all of you study hard, help out with the household chores, and take care of one other."

Robbie was about one month old the first time I was left alone to babysit him and the rest of my siblings. During this time, every weeknight all the adults in my family attended an English as a second language, or ESL, class to improve their English proficiency. It was on one of these evenings that I had my first experience of caring for all four of my younger siblings alone. It was a very windy night, gusts howling loudly and rustling the trees so that it sounded like someone was lurking outside our door and windows. We all got scared and went to hide inside the closet. I held Robbie tightly in my arms as we whispered to each other in the pitch dark.

"Did you hear that noise?" Betty asked. "Is that someone trying to break into the house?"

"I'm scared," Jane said. "What if they come in and kidnap us?"

I was frightened too, but tried to be reassuring. "It's just the wind."

After a short while, Robbie let out a piercingly loud cry and pooped in his diaper. The stench was so bad that we all had to vacate the closet. I placed Robbie on the bed and ran to fetch a clean cloth diaper. Meanwhile, he squirmed, flailed his arms and legs, and continued to scream at the top of his lungs. I eyed the two huge safety pins that secured Robbie's diaper, but had no idea how to remove them. I was terrified that I might poke Robbie and hurt him. I called Betty over and asked her to hold Robbie's legs down while I quickly figured out how to unfasten and remove the safety pins. Betty and I worked together as a team and somehow managed to change Robbie's diaper without hurting him or soiling ourselves.

We were so relieved after it was all over that we exchanged a huge smile of accomplishment. We did exactly what our parents wanted us to do—we worked as a team to take care of one another and did what was necessary to help our family survive and thrive in America.

The process of acculturation has provided my siblings and me with many valuable gifts. My parents' emphasis on our family's "team spirit" has fostered a special bond between my siblings and me. We work well together, are incredibly close, and are fiercely supportive and protective of one other.

My parents' examples of perseverance and resilience, as they faced significant professional and economic downward mobility, modeled for us how to rise above life's challenges while maintaining one's dignity, kindness, and optimism. Seeing our parents struggle in the early years instilled in us the importance of lending a hand to those who are less fortunate. Our parents' many sacrifices and hardships also nurtured in us the desire and determination to excel academically and professionally. I'm proud of all my siblings. Each one paid their own way through school and each is successful in their respective field. Betty is a civil engineer. Jane is a social worker. Kathy is a manager in the field of human resources. And Robbie is a fire captain.

I'm also forever grateful to my dad for standing strong and maintaining his dignity in the face of racial hatred. His courage and strength taught me the importance of treating everyone with respect regardless of their race, creed, profession, or sexual preference. Our family's hardships also ignited an enduring sense of humility, gratitude, and pride for everything we overcame to make it to the U.S. and all the sacrifices my parents made to give us political freedom and a better life.

Because of this, I've never been ashamed of my family's humble beginnings in America. I've used these adversities as a reminder and motivator to persevere and persist in the pursuit of my life's aspirations.

CHAPTER 12

New Kids in School

On our second day in Lafayette, several of the women from our sponsoring church took my mom, Betty, and me to a department store to get school clothes. I was captivated by the vastness of the store, the huge number of items available for sale, and how nicely everything was displayed. The distinct smell of new clothes filled me with excitement. Betty and I each received two new long dresses, a pair of shoes, and several pairs of knee-high socks.

The school we would be attending was a private Christian school, which had a strict dress code. Girls were allowed to wear only dresses, with a required length of at least three inches below the knee. Since the weather was cold, my mom decided that it was better to get dresses that were even longer to keep us warm.

The day after our shopping trip, Betty and I began school. On the morning of our first day, I had butterflies in my stomach as the two of us put on our new dresses, shoes, and socks. I wondered what it would be like to attend school in America. My mom packed a brown bag lunch for each of us, and we were driven to school by Mrs. O. Betty and I were both placed into the first grade, since neither of us spoke any English. In those days, there were no English as a second language classes or other resources for non-English speakers in schools.

Once we arrived at the school, Mrs. O escorted Betty and me to our classroom early so we could get acquainted with our new teacher, a young Caucasian woman named Mrs. F. She immediately showed us to our desks and gestured for us to sit down. Luckily, we were seated next to each other. Once we sat down, Mrs. F asked Betty her name.

Because Betty and I were informed of our new American names just days before starting school, we hadn't had the opportunity to learn how to pronounce or spell them yet. Betty looked at the floor, lowered her head, and remained silent as tears streamed down her flushed face. Mrs. F looked puzzled and slightly irritated when she saw Betty's tearful reaction to her question. Understanding that Betty was frightened and overwhelmed by the situation, I felt horrible for my sister and protective of her. I was also upset with Mrs. F for her lack of empathy and patience, so I jumped in and responded crossly, "Betty!"

"How do you write it?"

I shook my head vigorously when Mrs. F put her pencil to a piece of paper, gesturing to Betty to answer the question.

A tense, awkward silence hovered over us as Mrs. F continued to stare at my sister, making it obvious that she was awaiting a verbal reply. Betty responded by bursting out crying and putting her head down on the desk. Mrs. F finally backed off and walked away to do something else while I put my arms around Betty and tried to console her until the other kids came into the classroom.

Betty and I encountered many such obstacles as we tried to learn English, communicate, comprehend school lessons, make new friends, and adjust to American society and culture.

One of the remarkable things about our experience at the new school was that Betty and I were the only kids of color there. This caused us to stand out and made us targets of the children's scrutiny and teasing. While it was only natural for our schoolmates to be curious about people they perceived as different, the incessant hyper-focus on us and our behaviors made us feel marginalized and unwelcome. Kids came up to Betty and me to touch and squeeze our hair, faces, arms, and legs. Others made fun of us and laughed at how we spoke to each other in Vietnamese, or when we tried to speak English. While I was similarly intrigued by some of these kids, especially those who had blue or green eyes or red or blonde hair, I didn't dare think of touching them or getting in their faces.

When I saw dental braces for the first time, I was frightened by them. In those days, they sometimes included a contraption worn on the head, which had hooks that connected to the braces in the wearer's mouth. I wondered whether these kids had special powers, since I imagined that the wires might have electric currents running through them.

Incrementally over the first six months, our encounters with novel situations and the kids' teasing subsided, and Betty and I gradually acclimated to our new school. Still, learning a new language, understanding class instructions, and doing schoolwork proved to be a painfully slow, arduous, and frustrating process. I had to look up every single English word in my paperback English-Vietnamese dictionary to communicate, read, and complete class assignments. It was my constant companion on the playground as well as in the classroom. The pages of my dictionary became frayed from such constant use. Each homework assignment took an hour or more to complete. The considerable time consumed by homework was particularly challenging, since I also had daily responsibility for taking care of my siblings and completing many household chores.

I especially detested any history or writing assignment, because it involved not only looking up many words to understand the text but composing sentences and paragraphs to complete the assignment. In contrast, I loved the math tests and homework assignments, and easily breezed through those—unless they were word problems. I was considerably more advanced in math than my classmates since the material was a review of what I'd already learned in Vietnam. I was always the first one to finish all the math tests and usually received a perfect score.

Within two months of starting school, I was moved up into the second grade, and then the third. By the end of the school year, I no longer had to look up every word in my dog-eared dictionary, and my learning flowed more smoothly.

Before that, however, my experiences in third grade proved to be challenging, in many ways. I had no friends, since I'd entered the class midyear and didn't know any of the other kids. My English was quite rudimentary, which made communicating with the other kids difficult. And that made me feel alone and left out at first. Fortunately, after a few months, a kind classmate approached and asked me to hang out with her. Susie was bold and not afraid to befriend a student of a different race who barely spoke any English. Her easygoing personality and warmth helped me to learn not only English but also American culture. She invited me to her house for various social events and sleepovers. Her parents and older siblings were equally kind and welcoming, which gave me positive exposure to a "typical" American Christian family. Susie's friendship and support were crucial in helping me cope with the trials and tribulations of that year.

The most difficult trial of third grade was my teacher, Miss D. She was a tall, chunky, unfriendly middle-aged woman who exuded sternness, coldness, unhappiness, and authority. Miss D rarely smiled and often yelled. She also used physical punishment to control and intimidate her pupils. If someone misbehaved in class, she would yell out their name, tell them to go in front of the class, and have them bend over. Then she would proceed to spank them in front of the entire class, using a thick wooden paddle. Understandably, such acts of physical punishment and the threat of them kept all of us students in line. And since I was still struggling to learn and speak English, Miss D's impatience and sternness left me in a constant state of fear.

My worst nightmare came true during my second week in the class, during recess. There was a disagreement about a ball. A girl came up to me and ripped the ball out of my hands as I was playing with it on my own. So I went up to her and took it back. This girl quickly ran to tell my teacher on me, and I couldn't speak fast enough to explain my side of the story. Miss D roughly pulled me by the arm into our empty classroom, told me to bend over, and promptly gave me at least five hard spanks. The pain was severe—my rear end felt like it was on fire and my head spun from dizziness. I felt deep humiliation and anger for being unjustly punished while not being able to defend myself. I swore to myself to work even harder to learn English so that I would never be put in such a compromising position again.

Several weeks later, during one of our mandatory weekly chapel services, I got a big surprise. At these services, we were expected to behave, sing, pray, recite Bible verses, and listen to the pastor's sermon. In the middle of the service that day, Miss D pulled me out of my seat and up onto the stage. Then she, the pastor, and three other teachers placed me in the center of a circle they formed around me. They proceeded to put their hands over me and pray for what felt like an eternity. I began to sweat profusely as feelings of faintness and terror gripped me. I understood nothing that was going on, but I remember hearing the phrase "accept Jesus Christ as your Lord and Savior." After a while, I was taken off the stage and returned to my seat in the pews.

But the ordeal didn't end there. At the end of the service, I was taken by Miss D to an empty room adjacent to the chapel. I waited there silently while she and another teacher conversed excitedly to each other, saying more words I didn't understand. I grew more scared by the minute, wondering why I was being kept in the room and what they were going to do to me next. Once the students settled into their respective classes, these two teachers paraded me around the school, taking me into every single classroom. Upon our entry into each class, one of the teachers would make a joyous and high-pitched announcement, which included the phrase, "accepted Jesus Christ as her Lord and Savior." Each pronouncement was followed by clapping and cheers by everyone in the classroom. The whole time I was marched around the school, I had a knot in my stomach, a lump in my throat, and my body was petrified with fear. At the same time, I was afraid to express any negative feelings, for fear that I might be punished even more by Miss D.

Immediately after I got home, I told my mother what had happened to me at school, crying the whole time. My mom was upset and alarmed by what she'd heard. That evening, she spoke to my dad the minute he came home from work. Then they quickly went over to our sponsors' house to talk with them and express their disapproval about the way I was treated at school.

They asked our sponsors to relay to the school that we were Catholic, and therefore, "we do believe in Christ." My parents also emphasized that it was disrespectful and unethical for the school to "save" me without talking to them first. Our sponsors were equally troubled by what had happened and assured my parents that they would communicate their concerns to the school the following day.

The next evening, our sponsors came over to tell my parents that they'd talked to the school principal and he had apologized for upsetting them. The principal explained that the school meant no harm in "saving" me and that their intentions were good. Nonetheless, he reassured my parents, no such incidents would ever happen again. And they didn't.

Thankfully, the rest of my year in third grade proceeded without further drama. Miss D minimized her contact with me after the "saving" incident, which was a relief—I was grateful not to have more interaction with her. I focused on schoolwork and my friendship with Susie, and managed to thrive in school.

One weekday morning, my siblings and I awoke to an amazing sight—snowfall. We had never seen snow before. We were very excited and immediately ran outside to touch the snow. It was magical and exciting to see snowflakes falling from the sky and everything becoming covered in white. (Later we found out that it hadn't snowed in Lafayette for thirty years.)

Betty and I were even more ecstatic when we were told the schools were closed and we could stay home that day. After a quick breakfast, we all dressed up in our warmest clothes and went outside to play in the snow. For hours we made snowballs, stuck out our tongues to taste the snowflakes, and even managed to build a snowman. We played in the snow until our hands and noses felt frozen.

Several months later, Miss D announced at the beginning of class that a group of school parents were giving us a "special hot dog lunch surprise" that very day. My classmates all clapped and cheered. Since I had no idea what a hot dog was, I looked up the words *hot* and *dog* in my English-Vietnamese dictionary. I was frightened at first when I read the Vietnamese translations of those two words. Even though dog meat is a delicacy in Vietnam, I had never eaten it. I planned ways in my mind to decline the "hot dog" politely when it was presented to me, and instead show my teacher the brown bag lunch my mom had packed for me.

I was relieved but still curious when the hot dogs were finally handed out, since they didn't resemble a dog that was hot. Then I saw how much my classmates enjoyed this food, so I decided to try it. I took one small bite and thought it tasted all right. I ate my packed lunch and brought the remainder of the hot dog home to show my parents.

That evening, my father spoke to our sponsors about this food and learned that it contained no dog meat. Hot dogs, he learned, were actually a very common and popular food in the United States.

It was a big relief to learn that Americans didn't eat dog meat. We all got a good laugh.

——— ∞ ———

Betty and I finished our first year at the Christian school and graduated to become second and fourth graders, respectively. But then, in the spring of the following year, our family experienced a sudden and devastating loss. My maternal grandmother was tragically killed in a car accident on Mother's Day, 1977.

I was awakened by my mom's moaning and wailing, "Oh my God! I can't believe this! I can't believe she's really dead!"

My grandmother was being driven down to Los Angeles to visit her own mother for Mother's Day by one of my adoptive uncles. The car they were in caught on fire in Bakersfield at three in the morning. It was suspected that the car malfunctioned due to a defective part. My aunt was sitting beside my adoptive uncle in the front seat, while my grandmother sat in the backseat by herself, saying the rosary. The car went up in flames so quickly that people were unable to save her.

Her sudden death was a shock and a horrible loss for all of us, especially for my two youngest uncles, who were eleven and thirteen years old at the time. My grandmother was only fifty years old when she died.

We all lamented that she hadn't had the opportunity to enjoy her life in America. She had worked so hard in Vietnam as a grocery store owner, given birth to eleven children, and had single-handedly, heroically, led them through their numerous escapes throughout North and South Vietnam during the war. Her courage and ingenuity kept her children safe and saved them from death many times.

I'm thankful that in Vietnamese culture, we celebrate death anniversaries. On these occasions, our entire extended family comes together to celebrate the person who has passed on and share what they meant to us. Since my grandmother passed away on Mother's Day, we always gather on that day to visit her grave, say a prayer, share a meal at one of her children's homes, and enjoy our various memories of her. Even though she is no longer with us, she lives on in us and inspires us with her strength and courage.

CHAPTER 13

The Teacher Who Gave Me Hope

By the end of fifth grade, I was thriving socially and academically. Then, in early November of 1978, my parents bought our first home in America: a single-story fixer-upper with three bedrooms and one bathroom. This new house was about ten miles from where we'd been living, which meant that Betty and I had to change schools. While I was happy that my parents could purchase a home, I was sorry to be uprooted again from my school and friends.

I began the sixth grade at Hillcrest Elementary School midyear. The first six months at my new school and home were dominated by feelings of emptiness and sadness. In the fall and winter, the weather was always cold, sometimes foggy, and the sky was usually gray. Our new home felt cramped, old, and uninviting.

My experience at school was equally unpleasant. My classmates were unwelcoming and hostile from the start. When I arrived, two months into the school year, they had already formed social cliques, and none of them made any attempt to befriend me. In fact, they bullied me relentlessly from the very first day. They made fun of the way I looked, walked, and dressed. Thankfully, I was fluent in English by then, so at least they couldn't tease me for the way I talked.

With one Hispanic girl, my sixth-grade class was marginally more diverse than fifth grade had been; however, I was still the only Asian student in the class. We all came from working-class families, but the rest of the students were Caucasian.

I was told to go back to where I came from many times and was called various names: "chink," "jap," "gook," "retard," "boatperson," and even "street person"—the latter because my family was very poor at the time and one of my two pairs of pants was so big that I had to tie a rope around my waist to hold them up. (Unfortunately, my parents didn't know yet that there were second-hand stores where they could have purchased more changes of clothing for me and my siblings.)

Since our family income was under the poverty level, I qualified for free lunches, which gave my classmates another reason to ridicule me. In those days, kids who received free meals had to present a bright yellow card to the lunch lady in the cafeteria line. This also made me stand out as a target other kids labeled "freeloader" or "beggar."

The long-term effects of polio caused me to walk with a limp, which of course further fueled my classmates' incessant teasing and cruelty. They imitated and exaggerated my "funny walk," and I was always the last one to be picked for teams during physical education. The team captain that was "stuck with me" usually made his displeasure known by sighing loudly and announcing, "We have the cripple!"

———— ❧ ————

One day at recess I was on the monkey bars by myself when a boy came by and yanked my ankle, causing me to fall hard onto the ground. In the process, he also broke the strap on my shoe, rendering it useless. I panicked, worried about how my parents would be able to afford another pair of shoes, and slapped the boy in the face. Then I walked straight into the office to notify the principal. The boy was called in by the principal and his mom was notified about the infraction. In the meantime, I had to go shoeless for the rest of the day while enduring the kids' anger that I had told on one of their friends.

The bullying caused me to lose my appetite and develop insomnia. Each weekday morning, I woke up with a stomachache or headache. I told my parents many times that I was ill and couldn't go to school, but I never told them about the bullying at school, no matter how bad it was. I figured they had enough to worry about—working multiple jobs and putting in long hours to support me and our family of seven.

In the midst of all this, I somehow managed to continue to perform all my household duties and care for my younger siblings, while also excelling in school. I tested into the Mentally Gifted Minor Program that year and was given free rein to explore my academic abilities. This program was designed to allow students to progress at their own pace—to advance in the various academic subjects as quickly and as far as they were capable. Schoolwork became my lifeline. I immersed myself in it and challenged myself to outperform all my classmates. I kept myself busy by engrossing myself in whatever subject I was learning, with the goal of advancing to the next level as soon as possible. Being razor-focused on school gave me a purpose and made being friendless and stigmatized less painful.

I also coped with the bullying by immersing myself into a world of fantasy. I became obsessed with the television show *The Bionic Woman* and watched it daily after school. The heroine was a medically reconstructed woman who received "bionic" (enhanced prosthetic) ears and legs after an accident. She used the superhuman powers the devices gave her to fight crime and help others. Watching this show helped me escape from the reality of having an embarrassing limp and being bullied. I'd imagined that maybe someday I too could get bionic legs, which would rid me of my limp and give me the opportunity to carry out good deeds for humanity.

———❦———

Although my experiences in sixth grade were difficult, a great blessing of that year was my teacher, Mr. Bruno. He was kind and gentle, and his height, thinness, and beard reminded me of Abraham Lincoln. He recognized my classmates' cruelty towards me and did his best to intervene on my behalf whenever he saw them mistreating me. In those days, there wasn't the knowledge or awareness we have today of the negative effects of bullying, and teachers weren't trained on how to handle such situations. Nonetheless, Mr. Bruno did notice what was happening and took the time to give me support and encouragement. Whenever he saw that I was particularly down, he'd pull me aside to talk with me and made it a point to express his belief in me.

"Don't pay attention to them," he would say. "They're just jealous. You're a good person and a smart student. Keep up the good work and don't let anything stop you from doing your best!"

Mr. Bruno's kindness and reassuring words gave me hope. His empathy and belief in me made a huge difference and changed the trajectory of my life. I was at a crossroads during a very difficult period—at risk of giving up on life and going down a self-destructive path. I had suicidal thoughts: *How nice it would be if a car hit me as I crossed the street. Then I would no longer have to endure the daily bullying.*

Mr. Bruno's kind gestures prevented me from things like hanging out with the wrong crowd—the "stoners" who didn't care about school, often cut class, and smoked weed. Thank God they didn't want to be my friends, because I might have joined them if they had; I was so desperate for any sense of belonging and kindness from my classmates. Mr. Bruno's attention and caring kept me on the straight and narrow and contributed to my success in school.

Fortunately for our family, Mr. Bruno was not only kind to me, he was also wonderful to my younger siblings, who had him as their teacher as well. Our entire family benefitted from Mr. Bruno's compassion and dedication as a teacher.

With Mr. Bruno and my parents in sixth grade (1978).

Mr. Bruno's support made all the difference in my life, as I'm sure it did in countless other students'. Being a teacher is one of the noblest professions. Most of us have benefitted from the kindness and dedication of at least one special teacher. I want to thank our teachers for caring, for staying late, for teaching us not only about school subjects but also about life, for spending your own money to buy school supplies, for your belief in us, for your words of encouragement and wisdom when we are downtrodden, and for giving us hope when we need it the most.

⁃⦵⦵⦵⁃

As painful as my sixth grade experiences were, they revealed something significant. In the depths of my anxiety and depression, I somehow managed to excel academically while also fulfilling my household responsibilities. The gift of this adversity was discovering my own resilience. There was within me an inner strength and resourcefulness that enabled me to cope, mobilize, survive, and thrive even in the darkest of times.

This is the paradox of adversity. Going through life's most difficult challenges can reveal our greatest strengths and resilience.

CHAPTER 14

Teenage Rebellion

Things changed for the better in the spring of sixth grade, when I got a "Farrah Fawcett" haircut from a family friend who was a hairstylist, for free. It was the new fad haircut for girls at the time, and everyone coveted it. Overnight, I became one of the "popular girls" in school. The other kids stopped bullying me. Everyone wanted to be my friend.

It's mind-blowing how superficial kids can be. Several of the popular boys even asked me to be their girlfriend. I declined. My parents had pounded into my head that I couldn't have a boyfriend until I was at least in college. Besides, I was too busy to have a boyfriend, given my schedule of homework, chores, and caring for my siblings. Nonetheless, I was grateful that the bullying stopped, and I enjoyed the positive attention from my classmates. My depression and anxiety lifted immediately after the bullying ended, and the last several months of sixth grade went smoothly.

My transition into middle school, Glenbrook Junior High, was seamless, and I developed a good group of friends there. Though these friends were from a "tough crowd," I felt at home with them. It was a culturally diverse group of kids—Hispanic, African American, and Filipino—and I was thankful for the cultural and ethnic diversity I found, in contrast to my overwhelming white elementary schools.

With these friends behind me, while I didn't pick on kids or start fights unprovoked, if someone looked at me the wrong way or tried to start something, I didn't hesitate to get in their face and tell them off.

One time, a girl from another tough crowd challenged me to a fight after school. I showed up and fought her while a huge bunch of kids watched. This poor girl suffered all the rage I'd stored up against all the kids who'd ever bullied me. I pounded her with my fist and scratched her face and arms with my long nails. She ran away within five minutes. Suffice it to say, after this one-sided brawl, no one messed with me again. I'd earned a reputation as a tough girl.

I used that tough girl persona to help others that year. When two newly arrived Vietnamese refugee kids began attending my school and were being bullied as I had been, I went after the bullies. I told them to stop harassing the Vietnamese kids or they'd have to deal with me and my friends.

While being a part of this group was great for me at school, it made me more rebellious towards my parents at home. I began wearing makeup, which my mom strongly opposed and made every attempt to confiscate from me. My solution was to hide my makeup and put it on only at school. I also struggled with my ethnic identity and chose to emulate my Hispanic friends. I even began speaking English with a Mexican accent. In the photos of me taken during this period, I strongly resemble a Chicana in the way I dressed, wore my hair, and did my makeup. I also began to converse more in English and less in Vietnamese at home. In response, my parents instituted a behavioral modification program designed to ensure that my siblings and I would maintain our fluency in Vietnamese. Each time any of us spoke English at home, we had to put five cents into a glass jar.

I also rebelled against being saddled with so many household responsibilities. I was expected to pick up my younger siblings immediately after school, take care of them, do housework, cook meals for the family, and get good grades. I felt shackled by my family obligations.

Even worse was the fact that I couldn't go anywhere without my siblings. Whenever I asked for permission to attend a school dance or a party, my parents' usual reply was, "You can go if you take all your siblings with you." Of course, I'd end up not going—because who'd want to do that! I was mad at my parents for not understanding my need to have friends and my desire to spend time with them. But given how tough my friends were, maybe this was my parents' way of protecting me from kids they perceived as "troubled."

My parents' limitations on my social life, and my resentment towards them for what I perceived as their overreliance on me, caused many arguments and clashes. A couple of times, these intergenerational conflicts became so severe that they escalated into loud shouting matches. These skirmishes caused me to withdraw more and more from my parents, which in turn made them feel like they were losing me. This prospect was particularly worrisome for them since they believed my rebelliousness would most likely rub off on my siblings and cause them to misbehave as well. My parents often told me, "You are the head of the ship. You must set a good example for your siblings. If you misbehave and make bad choices, your siblings will do the same."

Eventually all this conflict led to my parents confiding in Father D, a new priest at our church. He was a marriage and family therapist who was pursuing a PhD in clinical psychology and theology at UC Berkeley. Father D was at our house on most days. He counseled me to "straighten me out," and sometimes helped me with my schoolwork. He met with me individually at least once a week and taped some of our "therapy" sessions. One of the sessions occurred immediately after I had gotten into a bad argument with my mom. Father D taped me saying that I hated my mom. Right after my session, he met alone with my mom and had her listen to what I had said.

To be clear, what Father D did was highly unethical and unprofessional. He should not have taped our sessions without explicit permission from me and my parents. Moreover, he was wrong to betray my trust by having my mom listen to something that was shared in confidence and spoken in a moment of anger. The strict standard of ethical conduct for therapists treating teenagers is that all communications shared by the teen to the therapist need to be kept confidential from the parents, unless the teen is at risk to herself, others, or is involved in a situation that involves abuse. This policy should be communicated to the parents and the teen at the outset of treatment and applies even if the therapist is providing the therapy free of charge, which he was. Furthermore, Father D's overinvolvement with our family, blurring the lines of professional versus personal, should have been a big red flag, as it is a cardinal sin within the therapeutic profession.

Unfortunately, neither my parents nor I knew any of this at the time. My parents were simply grateful to Father D when they noticed that my defiance began to decrease. Towards the end of seventh grade, I was again an obedient and deferential child. That's when I began thinking about my future. Since I wanted to go to college, but neither I nor my parents had the money, I got a job. Every Saturday, I began to clean houses, and my parents put all my earnings into a savings account, earmarked for my education.

In the eighth grade, I became student body president and applied to get into a college prep high school. I wanted to make sure that I had a good foundation to excel in college and maximize my chances of getting scholarships. The admissions process for this prestigious high school included an admissions test and an in-person interview with the principal, Sister Ann. My mom came with me to the interview and did most of the talking, despite a case of laryngitis that had her struggling to answer the questions in a raspy voice. She told Sister

Ann about my history with polio and about the strong will and determination she saw in my eyes when I pulled myself up in the crib at the age of three. She also told her about our refugee experience and what a good child I was: how I took care of all my siblings, cooked, and cleaned—how I was my siblings' "second mother."

When Sister Ann asked me why I wanted to attend her school, my response was, "I really want to go to college, but I know my parents can't afford to pay for it. Because of this, I have to go to a good high school, so I can increase my chances of getting a college scholarship."

In the spring of eighth grade, I was informed of my acceptance to this college prep high school. I received a partial scholarship, but to pay the rest of my tuition I would do work-study every day after school (cleaning classrooms and the library) and continue to work as a housekeeper on the weekends.

While I was still in eighth grade, I received a wonderful surprise. My old elementary school had closed down, and Mr. Bruno had transferred to Glenbrook. It was wonderful to see him again (under much-improved circumstances), and better yet, I was able to work in his class as his teacher's aide. I thrived both socially and academically that year, and became far happier and more confident.

CHAPTER 15

The Betrayal—#MeToo

ather D had come into our lives in the fall of 1980, when I was thirteen years old and in the seventh grade. One Sunday, on our way home from church after meeting the new priest, my mom spoke enthusiastically to my dad: "Father D's sermon was just wonderful! He's so charismatic. He reminds me of Father Ky—it's amazing how much they resemble one another. It's as if Father Ky has returned to us again!"

All of these things were true. Father D did have an uncanny resemblance to Father Ky, the cousin who convinced my mom's parents to let my mom and dad marry. They both wore glasses, had the same hairline, and were even from the same Franciscan order. And he did have a magnetic personality. All the parishioners commented on how inspirational and moving his sermons were and what a wonderful addition he was to our church community. Father D was Asian and appeared to be in his late thirties. And, as mentioned, he was a licensed therapist and working on a PhD.

Very soon after we first met him, when I was just beginning the seventh grade, Father D began to pay a lot of attention to me. This was after my parents confided in him about my "acting out" behaviors— being argumentative and rebellious—and he began the individual therapy sessions to make me an obedient child again. For this, as well as his resemblance to Father Ky, Father D quickly earned my parents' trust and admiration.

In our devoutly Catholic family, a priest was next to God. Father D's wittiness, charisma, and stirring sermons made him the favorite priest in our church and in my family. My parents and our extended family felt honored that he "favored" our family, and he called us his adoptive family, since he too was originally from Asia. In fact, my entire extended family, including my maternal grandfather, aunts, uncles, and cousins, were so enamored and trusting of him that they encouraged one of my aunts to see him as a therapist. One of my younger sisters and my parents themselves also received therapy from him periodically.

Later in my own career, I learned that therapists are strictly forbidden from such behaviors. Father D violated ethical guidelines for therapists when he had a "dual relationship" with our family—being our priest and friend while simultaneously seeing multiple members of my family as clients.

In June of 1981, when I was fourteen years old, Father D told my parents that it would be a "good educational experience" for me to take a six-week road trip with him from California to Oregon, Washington, and Yellowstone National Park, and then on to Canada: Banff and Jasper National Parks in Alberta, and Victoria, in British Columbia. This trip was presented as a "graduation gift" to reward me for my excellent performance in academics, my successful leadership as the student body president of my junior high school, and winning the first prize in a districtwide essay contest. (My principal was so proud that the winning essay came from our school that he had me read my essay at the end-of-the-year awards ceremony.)

Since Father D had always been generous, kind, and caring towards our family, my parents were grateful that he offered to take me on this special trip. They trusted him implicitly and told me it would be a good learning experience for me—and when would I ever have the opportunity to see so many places at once? Given my family's financial limitations, my parents could never have afforded to take my siblings and me on such an excursion. So it was decided that Father D and I would leave at the end of June for the road trip.

We departed as planned, driving in Father D's brown Thunderbird from one remote campground to the next, and sharing a two-person tent at night.

About a week into the trip, we were driving in the car when he asked me what I wanted to eat for lunch. "Something different," I said. "Not peanut butter jelly sandwiches again. I'm sick of them."

Father D wasn't happy with my answer. He became irate and yelled at me. "You are so ungrateful and rude! Just wait till I tell your parents about this when we get home. How do you think they'll react, huh? You'd better behave, or they'll be hell to pay when you get home!"

After this, he gave me the silent treatment for over twenty-four hours. I tried repeatedly to apologize to him for my comment, but he responded with a stone-cold face and total silence. This incident baffled and frightened me. I also felt betrayed. Who was this person I was traveling with? I'd never seen Father behave this way before. He used to be so nice and funny. Now he was stern and punitive. I would never have agreed to go on the trip if I'd known he would be this way. Under the circumstances, I had little choice but to behave and be careful not say anything that might upset him. After this incident, I tried my best to be very respectful and obedient towards him.

A couple of days later, his car broke down and we had to stop to get it fixed at a garage. Suddenly, he lashed out at me: "You're so selfish to whine about what we eat! Do you see what I have to spend to fix this car?"

Late on a Saturday night in the second week of the trip, I was woken from a deep sleep in the pitch-dark tent by the feeling of a grown man lying on top of me, kissing me very hard on the mouth and biting my upper lip.

Oh my God, what's happening? I thought. *Is this some aggressive crazy intruder? Where's Father D? Did this guy kill him?*

I felt trapped and couldn't breathe—the intruder had covered my entire mouth with his. I wrenched my head to the side, gasping for air. Then I saw that the biting, angry man on top of me was—*oh my God!*—Father D.

I immediately began crying and shaking uncontrollably. Within moments, Father D pulled away from me and said, "It's okay. It's okay. Stop crying!"

But I couldn't stop. My entire body trembled convulsively as I sobbed. At one point, he moved in closer and tried to put his arms around me tightly. I pushed him away, turned to the other side, and curled into a fetal position, trying to shut him out. I cried until I fell asleep again.

The following morning, I woke early. Father D was still asleep. My upper lip was swollen, and I tasted blood. My eyes were puffy. I sat up and quickly left the tent, hoping I could find somebody to help me. But there was no one around. I didn't see any homes or ranger stations nearby. Our campsite was completely empty, surrounded by miles of forested land. And in those days, there were no cell phones.

A few minutes later, Father D came out of the tent and sat down at the picnic table.

"Come sit next to me," he said.

I sat down and he moved so close to me that the entire left side of his body was touching my right side. I felt uncomfortable and claustrophobic. I tried to move away but he scooted right back up next to me.

"I apologize for what happened last night," he said in a quiet voice. "It will never happen again."

I said nothing.

Then he told me to go back into the tent so that he could celebrate mass with me, since it was Sunday. I obeyed and walked into the tent, feeling apprehensive and dejected.

"Don't tell anyone about what happened last night," he said again at the end of mass. "God wants you to obey this command!"

After this, we went back outside to the picnic table and he poured me a small bowl of cereal for breakfast. I couldn't eat. Each bite of food came right back up whenever I swallowed. Seeing this, he reminded me that I needed to eat because my "body was the temple of God" and I needed to take care of it. I said nothing, went back into the tent, and slept for the remainder of the day.

In the middle of the night, I was startled awake by the sound of my own crying and screaming. I bolted upright, my heart racing, drenched in sweat. I'd had a nightmare. In it, I was desperately running away from a man who was chasing after me. The man resembled Father D. He caught up with me, pinned me to the ground, and ripped off my shirt. Then I woke up.

The following morning, we packed up and he drove us to the next destination. I was silent for the next two days, crying off and on. I felt trapped, scared, and violated.

Several days after he'd initially abused me, I was showering in the ladies' bathroom when I heard him outside yelling my name: "Carolee, Carolee, are you in there?" I could hear the urgency and panic in his voice. "What's taking you so long? Hurry up!"

He was probably worried that I had met someone and confided in them about what he'd done to me. After this, he told me I had to limit my shower time to five minutes. I was also forbidden to talk to anyone in the bathroom, and he always waited outside while I showered.

About a week after this, I was again in a deep slumber when Father got on top of me and began kissing me. This time he also stuck his tongue inside my mouth and fondled my breasts. My throat tightened and I gagged reflexively. I gasped for air and tried to push him off of me. This made him angry. He responded by holding me down. "Hold still," he yelled at me. "Stop resisting!"

He continued to kiss and fondle me until he was finished satisfying himself. I don't recall what he did, because I dissociated—my mind became detached from my body and I went into another realm to escape from what was happening.

Afterwards, I grew more afraid and discouraged. The fact that he didn't keep his promise to stop assaulting me made me worried. I thought to myself, *I'm out here in nowhere—who can help me? Even if I saw someone, would they believe me if I told them what was happening?*

In fact, he specifically told me many times that no one would believe me if I told.

"I wouldn't bother telling anyone if I were you. There's no way anybody would believe a child like you over me. I'm a good priest. You see how everyone loves and respects me?"

I came to accept that what Father D said was probably right, and this made me feel helpless and despondent. I no longer resisted. I submitted. The sexual abuse continued, recurring almost every day— sometimes both during the day and at night—for the rest of the trip. Whenever he satisfied himself, I again escaped into my mind and shut down.

On multiple occasions, I asked to call my parents. He repeatedly refused my requests, saying, "We are out here in nowhere; there are no pay phones here."

One time I spotted pay phones on the road and asked again. "It's too expensive," he snapped.

About four or five weeks into the trip, after having almost no contact with other people besides Father D, I grew more desperate to talk to my parents. I wept and pleaded with him. "Please let me call my parents. I have to talk to them!"

He finally relented—just this one time during the entire trip. He allowed me a very brief conversation with my parents at a gas station pay phone. But he coached me on exactly what to say beforehand and stood next to me while I spoke with them.

"Make it short. Tell them you're having a good time—that you're learning a lot and seeing a lot."

When I got on the phone with my parents, I parroted what he instructed me to say, suppressing a powerful urge to scream, *Please help me! Come get me!*

But I knew better.

Nonetheless, it felt so good to talk to my parents, to hear their voices, that I began to tear up. When Father saw this, he grabbed the phone away from me and began talking to my parents. "Carolee is having a great time," he assured them, "and learning a great deal."

The reality was that, though we drove through the various states, we saw only a few of the promised sites. Most of the time, we were in the tent at a secluded campsite, where he would first molest me and then lecture me on "God's teachings." He emphasized that God had chosen me to be his "special sheep." This meant that Father D and I were supposed "to take care of each other." If I obeyed and did exactly what God and Father commanded, my family and I would go to heaven. But if I told about our "special relationship" or resisted his requests and instructions, my family and I would go to hell. Being a rule follower and a devout Catholic, I believed everything he told me.

The only halfway bright spot on the trip was the Nancy Drew mysteries I had brought with me. I had received a set from our sponsors the previous Christmas and brought six of them with me. These books were a lifesaver! They allowed me another form of escape, into the world of fiction, which helped me cope with the ongoing emotional and sexual abuse.

———— ∞∞∞ ————

A few times during the trip, we did encounter other campers. Father instructed me to tell them that I was his niece. When I did talk with others, he was always within earshot to listen in on what I was saying. One time, a nice family invited us to have dinner with them. He quickly declined their offer.

After six weeks, the trip finally came to an end and we headed home. I was very relieved when I recognized the freeway and the exit that led to home. But we didn't drive there directly. Father D stopped at a park several blocks away from my house and turned off the ignition. He had his lecture prepared.

"Remember what I told you before about keeping our secret. You must obey God's commands and not tell anyone about our special relationship. God is merciful, but he'll send you and your family to hell if you disobey his commands. I wouldn't want that to happen to you. Hell is a forever place; you can't ever escape it once God puts you there … When you see your family, look happy and tell them you had a great time …"

By the time I walked into the house to reunite with my family, Father had brainwashed me into thinking that no one would ever believe that he was capable of molesting me. He was a powerful man who was loved and respected by everyone. I was convinced that God would banish me and my family to hell if I ever uttered a word about what had happened during the trip.

———— ∞∞∞ ————

100

After the trip, Father D continued to visit our family almost daily, and to sexually abuse me on a weekly basis. Somehow he'd gotten a key to my house, and he snuck in every Friday or Saturday night, while my family slept, to molest me. When I turned sixteen, the molestation escalated to full intercourse.

Thankfully, I had enough sense to get on birth control pills to protect myself from becoming pregnant.

At one point, Father even infiltrated my Catholic high school and gained access to me by volunteering as a therapist there. He befriended the head counselor and convinced her that my mom was "so controlling" that I needed weekly therapy at school with him in order to cope. Father told me this in advance and coached me to confirm this assertion with the head counselor in case she inquired about my relationship with my mom. Sure enough, a few days later, she had me come to her office and asked whether my mom was controlling. I told her I didn't think my mom was controlling, but we argued sometimes. After this, Father wrote weekly passes for me to be taken out of class, and he assaulted me during these "therapy sessions." This went on for about a year.

As he had done before, he taped the individual and family sessions my sister and I had with him, and he used the tapes to sow discord within my family and gain unrestricted access to me—and my siblings. For example, after he played the recording for my mom in which I'd said I hated her, my mom understandably, became upset and cried profusely. He "kindly" offered to take me and my siblings to his apartment in Berkeley for the weekend so that my mom could "have time to recover."

His work with my parents as their couple's therapist also reinforced their trust in him. He encouraged them to "have quality time together." To provide it, about once a month he took my siblings and me camping or to his apartment on the weekends.

On these occasions he usually gave Betty and me sweet wine and coaxed us to drink it. Other times, he hypnotized Betty, Jane, and me to see how willing we were to follow his commands. He claimed that he was learning these techniques in his psychology classes and needed to practice on us. He took me to the Psychology building at UC Berkeley multiple times to videotape our therapy sessions. I have no idea what he did with these videos. He also brought my siblings and me into his classes several times to demonstrate how he did family therapy with us for his classmates and professors.

In spite of the ongoing sexual abuse, I somehow managed to do well in my college prep high school. But the first year was really tough. I quickly discovered that my education up to that point hadn't adequately prepared me for the academic rigors of this new school. It made me question whether I had what it took to be at this elite institution. I was also adjusting to working two part-time jobs while trying to acquire good study habits and maintain my usual household responsibilities. I worked every day after school cleaning an art classroom and every Saturday as a housekeeper. The painstaking effort it took to develop more effective learning skills and master my classes reminded me of how it had felt to learn English when I first came to America. But in time, I did acclimate, and by the end of my first year I managed to get straight A's.

I felt out of place at my high school, an all-girls school, where most of the students came from affluent families. It was common to see people drive to school in a Porsche, BMW, or Mercedes Benz. When I was old enough to drive, I was lucky to have a car at all. My "vintage" 1973 Toyota Corolla had been rescued from a junkyard by my dad. He towed it home and rebuilt the engine, spending hours under the hood in the cold and rain to fix up the car for me.

In fact, for many years, my dad spent most weekends and week-nights after work fixing one or another of our family cars. They were all second- or thirdhand and frequently broke down. The mental image of him bent over under the hood still fills me with deep appreciation and sadness.

Even though my dad put many hours into repairing my car, it was still unreliable. About once a week, I'd have to pull to the side of the road, open the hood, and tinker with some part of the engine to get it running again. My dad always explained to me where the problems were and how to fix them. Given that there were no cell phones back then, and we didn't have the money to join AAA, it's a miracle that I managed to get around in that car for three years without a major incident.

My family's poverty set me apart from the handful of friends I'd made at school in other ways, as well. While they had the time to go to parties and hang out after school, I was usually rushing to one or another of my jobs, volunteering on Sundays as an activities' assistant at a convalescent home and a babysitter at a crisis nursery, and studying or taking care of my siblings. Nonetheless, my girlfriends were kind, welcoming, and put up with my unavailability. Even though I didn't see them as much as I would have liked, when we did get together, we had a lot of fun hanging out at one of the girls' houses to talk, watch movies, and listen to music.

My academic success and the camaraderie of my friends allowed me to project the image of a well-adjusted girl who had it all together. But underneath this facade, I was struggling. I was easily startled, hypervigilant, had chronic insomnia, and what little sleep I got was plagued by nightmares. These bad dreams were always like the one I'd had the night after Father D first assaulted me. I was being chased by a man, couldn't get away, and was sexually attacked.

To cope, I compartmentalized my world. My public self was high-achieving, dutiful, and "happy." My private world contained my relationship with Father D and the discomfort, guilt, shame, and many fears I had about not being able to safeguard "the secret." I continued to hide the fact that Father D was having sexual intercourse with me regularly. My private world made me feel isolated, helpless, and sad. I imagined various scenarios for how I might tell someone about what was happening, but I always chickened out.

Father D's deviousness and his influence in my family played a major role in maintaining my silence about the abuse. He manipulated my emotions using a combination of verbal threats coupled with frequent acts of kindness towards me and my family.

He took me and my siblings to movies, restaurants, performances, state parks, and sightseeing spots, as well as his house. And most of these outings were fun and enjoyable. He made my siblings and me feel special by telling us that we were his favorite kids and giving us "special treatment." He bought us small gifts and at times stepped in to purchase larger items that my parents couldn't afford. In one of my "sessions" with him at school, Father presented me with a winter jacket—something I needed but my parents didn't have the money to buy.

These apparent kindnesses were what made the whole situation so confusing for me. In those days, there was no public education about the dangers of sexual abuse—by priests or anyone else. So there was no way for me to know that what he was doing was inappropriate or wrong. At the same time, all the adults around me seemed to respect and even idolize Father D.

Father also provided me with helpful academic guidance and support. This was something I didn't have access to at home, given my parents' inexperience with the American school system. He sometimes helped me with my schoolwork and encouraged me to apply to my college prep high school, and later to UC Berkeley. His assistance in all these areas were crucial to my academic success. But he did these things to control and manipulate me, and make me more dependent on him. And, though I did not realize it at the time, I recognize now that he encouraged me to apply to UC Berkeley so he could continue to have access to me.

Collectively, all these manipulative acts disguised as altruistic gestures, his verbal threats, and his authority in our church and with my family, created the perfect conditions for Father D to continue to abuse me while I maintained my silence. Eventually, the relationship became normalized for me, something I accepted as part of my life.

Shortly after the "camping trip," I'd become obsessed with clowns and started collecting them. In hindsight, it's obvious that this was a veiled way of trying to communicate what was going on within me: *I was the clown.* I might look happy on the outside, but inside I harbored an ocean of stifled anguish. In many ways, my four years of high school were the loneliest and most difficult ones of my life.

But with a lot of hard work and determination—and compartmentalization—I managed to graduate from high school with highest honors and gained admission to UC Berkeley with a full-ride scholarship.

CHAPTER 16

Knowledge Opens Doors

I loved the stimulating academic and social experiences at UC Berkeley, and made some good friends at Hoyt Hall, the all-female co-op where I lived. The rent there was cheap; each student was required to do five hours of chores per week. I cooked one day a week and cleaned the bathrooms. I also joined the Vietnamese Student Association (VSA) and found it to be an invigorating experience. For the first time, I was surrounded by other Vietnamese refugee students who shared and understood the challenges my family and I went through.

The friends I made in this association were kind, driven, and hardworking. We recognized the importance and responsibility of excelling in school to provide a better future for ourselves and our families. During my time in the VSA, I held leadership positions and started multiple community-service programs. One of them involved reaching out to low-income Vietnamese high school students and providing them with tutoring and mentoring services. We talked to these students about the importance of going to college and arranged for them to tour UC Berkeley so they could have exposure to the university experience.

While I thrived socially and academically, I struggled with being away from my family. Since I was like my siblings' second mother, leaving them was excruciating. On the night my dad dropped me off at school for the first time, my siblings and I wept bitterly as we said our goodbyes. I felt like I was being ripped away from my kids. In fact, I referred to my siblings as my kids until I graduated from college.

Thankfully, my dad was still working in Berkeley at the foreign car parts company at the time, as co-manager with Lew. He came to pick me up every Friday night that first year so I could reunite with my siblings for the weekend. In hindsight, I believe that moving away to college reawakened the separation anxiety and post-traumatic stress I experienced during my escape out of Vietnam. Even though I was no longer in danger of losing my family, any separation from them triggered severe feelings of fear and loss.

Father D's involvement with my family continued until the middle of my first year at UC Berkeley. One weekend, while I was at home, my mom told me and my siblings that Father would no longer have any contact with us and wouldn't be coming to our house anymore. She did not explain why. Father's name was not mentioned again in my family for many years.

I later learned from my mother that she and my dad had met with Father shortly before her announcement and requested that he stop seeing our family. Evidently two people, one of whom was a priest, had warned my mom about Father, saying that he "shouldn't be around children." Someone else told my mom that he'd spotted Father "hugging and kissing" me at a park.

During the meeting, my parents asked Father directly whether he'd had a relationship with me. He vehemently denied it. In fact, he became irate and accused them of slander. He threatened to sue my parents if they ever said anything bad about him to anyone, especially after all he had done for our family. They left the meeting

107

feeling guilty and humiliated and feared they might have treated him unjustly by being overly cautious. But their relationship with him had ended.

Because I was unaware of all that had transpired between him and my parents, Father D continued to have access to me in Berkeley. He told me that while he was confused by my parents' request that he not to come to our house anymore, he would honor it. He emphasized that their request "saddened and hurt" him, since he loved us and always tried to do his best to help us. Father D was so convincing that I actually believed him and felt sorry for him. At the time, due to Father D's brainwashing, I believed that my relationship with him was consensual, albeit one I couldn't talk about because he was a priest.

Several other pivotal events finally transformed the nature of my relationship with Father D. In the spring of 1987, my second year in college, I was looking for a summer job and came across one that piqued my interest. It involved working as a peer counselor with refugee youths and their families in San Francisco. I went for an interview and was hired by the executive director of the Vietnamese Youth Development Center (VYDC).

My clients were Cambodian, Chinese, Lao, and Vietnamese refugee youths and their families who lived in the Tenderloin area. Although this neighborhood is known for its high crime rate and prostitution, the proximity to Chinatown and low-cost housing made it attractive to the Southeast Asian refugees. In my capacity as a peer counselor, I provided counseling, tutoring, summer job placements, and conducted psychoeducation and support groups for these youths and their families. All the services were tailored to promote the clients' ability to acculturate successfully into American culture and minimize the intergenerational conflicts between these youths and their parents. My work at VYDC was so eye-opening, meaningful, and rewarding that it inspired me to choose psychology as my college major.

That fall, when I returned for my third year of college, I declared psychology as my major and took two upper division courses: clinical psychology and Buddhist psychology. These classes transformed and saved my life. In Buddhist psychology, I learned how to meditate, which sparked my capacity to see things more clearly and allowed me to become more aware of my thoughts, feelings, and body. I immersed myself in the study of Buddhism and went on multiple Buddhist retreats taught by Thich Nhat Hanh and Pema Chodron. At the same time, I continued to attend weekly mass and a student discussion group at the Newman Center, a Catholic church in Berkeley that catered to college students. I was impressed and inspired by the progressiveness and openness I felt from the Jesuit priests there, as well as from the parishioners.

In clinical psychology, I learned about trauma, specifically the signs, symptoms, and psychological impact of sexual trauma on survivors. In one class discussion, my professor discussed case examples and the various tactics abusers used to intimidate, influence, and manipulate their victims. I began to wonder whether I was a victim of sexual abuse. By then, Father D had been abusing me for about six years.

In those days, most people, including myself, didn't have access to a home computer. Class papers were still being written on typewriters, and the World Wide Web did not exist yet, neither did Internet searches. Everything I learned about trauma and childhood sexual abuse came from my classes, books and articles, or television.

Several weeks after my clinical psychology professor's lecture on childhood traumas, I watched an episode of *Oprah* in which victims of childhood sexual abuse talked about their experiences of being groomed, manipulated, and abused by their perpetrators.

Their stories shook me to the core—I recognized myself! The next day, I called the student mental health center and requested an appointment. The following week, I entered therapy for the first time. I told my therapist only that I needed help getting out of a bad relationship.

When Father D found out, he strongly discouraged me from continuing. He asked me why I needed a therapist when I could talk to him. I told him I wanted "help dealing with stress" from a therapist who had experience working with other college students. He reluctantly conceded to "letting me" see the therapist but explicitly told me that I shouldn't divulge anything about our relationship. I was puzzled by his request and asked him why. He was evasive and became irritated with me for asking. Then he tried to guilt me, saying, "Do you want to get me into trouble?"

I said nothing but was perplexed by his reaction. I began to wonder: *Why would talking about our relationship get him into trouble? He knows that I'd never reveal to the therapist that he's a priest. If there's nothing wrong with our relationship, why does he want me to hide it from my therapist? And why would he discourage me from seeing a therapist when this is what* he *does for a living?*

His reaction to my being in therapy was a red flag to me that what he had been doing with me was wrong. After this initial conversation about my therapy, he strongly discouraged me from continuing and insisted that I tell him exactly what I discussed with my therapist. The more intrusive he became, the more convinced I was that I needed to get away from him. This realization was a turning point for me. To appease him, I lied and told him I had stopped seeing my therapist. But in reality, I continued to see her. I saw her as my best hope for getting out of the relationship.

With her support and guidance, I discovered that I was a strong person. She helped me to realize that I had the capacity to break free of him. She encouraged me to take baby steps by clarifying my goals, clearly stating my intentions to leave, and setting firm boundaries. But since I'd never told her how our relationship began, how old Father D was, or that he was a priest, she was operating largely in the dark.

I was still under his influence and still trying to protect him. In this nascent stage of understanding my own abuse, I didn't have the clarity or knowledge to recognize that he was still manipulating me to hide his criminal and unethical behaviors. In fact, I didn't even know that what he had done with me was a crime. My therapist never inquired whether there was coercion in the relationship, and I never volunteered the information.

Another factor that helped me leave Father D was my friendships with an amazing group of college girlfriends: Abbey, Angie, Lan, Lisa B, Lisa L, Maria H, Maria J, Phuong, and Yusing. These women were my "soul sisters," my greatest gifts from college! We were there for each other throughout college and have continued to support one another through all of life's trials and tribulations for the thirty-five years since. Their friendship and support helped me to grow as a person and empowered me to believe in myself. Even to them, though, I never divulged the true nature of my relationship with Father D—not until many years later, twenty-five years to be exact.

By the spring of 1988, I finally felt strong enough to tell Father D that I wanted out of the relationship. He resisted and talked me into "being friends" for a while. He said that it was "not natural or reasonable" for us to have a clean break, given that we'd "been together for so long."

I agreed initially, but then learned quickly that his idea of being friends didn't work for me. Father was still trying to treat me as if I was his girlfriend. Several weeks later, I told him I wanted out of the relationship entirely and didn't want to have any further contact with him. He responded by becoming needy, demanding, and possessive. He stalked me, called me incessantly, and told me that he wanted to leave the priesthood so he could marry me.

When I was in high school, he'd said that if I ever wanted to leave the relationship and date guys my own age he wouldn't stand in my way: "When that time comes, I'll just let you go so you can live your own life." It was yet another lie he'd told me, evidently.

Finally I threatened to report him to the police if he ever tried to contact me again. That worked.

In the end, it was the combination of my growing sense of self, my spirituality, the knowledge I'd gained from my psychology classes, the skills I'd learned in my therapy, and the love and support of my family and soul sisters that enabled me to finally extricate myself from Father D. It felt so incredibly liberating to finally break away from him after seven years. I wanted to put this part of my life behind me and bury it—so much so that it took almost five years before I told anyone about the abuse. I just wanted to move forward with my life and forget that any of it had ever happened to me.

———⚭———

My experience of "not telling" during my abuse and for many years after are all too common among survivors of childhood sexual abuse. This need to suppress the abuse speaks to the profound shame and pain survivors feel about the trauma. The burden of carrying the secrets of the trauma can be very harmful to our physical and mental health, as well as our sense of self. In contrast, speaking out about the trauma can be an extremely healing and liberating experience.

As a therapist and a survivor, I urge anyone whose abuse experience has negatively affected their life in any way to reach out for help.

Please remember that the abuse was not your fault and the shame is not yours to carry. It's entirely on the perpetrator. The power differential absolves you of responsibility—especially if you were a child when it happened. It doesn't matter what you did or felt at the time. Even if you enjoyed the attention, or liked nice things the abuser did for you or gave you, you did not deserve to be abused. Please get support and professional help so that you can begin to heal, so that your wounds of shame, sadness, fear, and helplessness can be transformed into the medals of resilience and courage that they truly are.

There is an interesting paradox to trauma. Even though traumatic events are difficult, they also allow us to discover our indomitable human spirit to survive and thrive in the face of adversity. We discover that the trauma did not destroy us. When we seek support, we show that we have the courage and the desire to heal. When we go through the healing process, we discover that we are strong. The fact that we are still here is a testament to our survival, tenacity, and resiliency.

I'm grateful that I survived my abuse and extricated myself from Father D. Some of the greatest gifts I've gained from my abuse include my empathy for others and my deep desire to help decrease suffering in whatever way I can. It began with my stumbling into my job at VYDC, which led me into the field of psychology and ultimately resulted in my becoming a psychologist. The gift of being able to accompany clients on their journey of healing is a great honor and a privilege. Each journey is unique, sacred, heart-wrenching, and powerful. Being able to bear witness to each person's pain, help them to process it, and then see them move on to live more fulfilling lives is deeply moving and inspiring.

The other gift that I gained from my trauma is learning the importance of self-care. Taking good care of ourselves facilitates our process of healing because it encourages us to tune into what we need—something that trauma survivors often struggle with. The conscious act of paying attention to our wants and needs facilitates our capacity to recognize that we are of value and gives us practice in nurturing ourselves.

I'm a big believer in self-care and have learned that when I take care of myself, everyone around me benefits, and everything in my work and personal life flows better. I emphasize to all my clients, regardless of whether they've had a trauma history or not, that self-care is one of the most important things we can do for ourselves and for others. It is *not* selfish to take care of ourselves. In fact, when we take the initiative to give ourselves what we need to live a happy and well-balanced life, everyone around us benefits from our positivity and health.

CHAPTER 17

Love and Devotion

About the time I was beginning to distance myself from Father D in 1987, the auto parts company that had employed my dad for fifteen years went bankrupt and had to lay him off. This had been my dad's only place of employment since his arrival to America. At the same time, my maternal grandfather was diagnosed with stage 4 lung cancer. My parents decided to move my grandfather in to live with them, and my dad became his caregiver.

When I came home to visit on the weekends, I witnessed my dad's total devotion to my grandfather. He took care of all my grandfather's daily needs without any show of resentment. This included feeding and bathing him, taking him to all his doctor's appointments, driving him to the park so he could feed the ducks, and cooking daily batches of herbal medicine that took half the day to make. My dad also sang and played the guitar to entertain my grandfather. If my mom was around, she usually joined in to sing while my dad played the guitar. These impromptu musical sessions always brought us joy and levity. My father cared for my maternal grandfather for nine months, until he passed away in August of 1988.

Seeing how my grandfather suffered from a myriad of symptoms associated with lung cancer made me afraid for my dad, since he too was a smoker. I pleaded with my dad to stop smoking, but he was unable to stop for any length of time. One day when I caught my dad sneaking a cigarette in the backyard, I broke down and cried. "I'm terrified of losing you to lung cancer."

"I can see that you're afraid," he said softly, looking me in the eyes. "I will stop."

From that day on, my dad never touched another cigarette. His determination to stop smoking was a testament to his love for me, my siblings, and my mother. It gave me hope that maybe he wouldn't die from lung cancer. More importantly, keeping his promise showed me that my thoughts and feelings mattered to him, that he loved his family and wanted to do whatever he could to be around for us. My dad's total devotion to our family, and his steadiness, gentleness, loving kindness, and willingness to do whatever it took to make us happy were some of the many reasons it was so easy to love him.

After my grandfather passed away, my dad got a job cleaning a twelve-theater multiplex in Daly City. The drive to work took an hour each way. By then, I was a junior at UC Berkeley but still came home on the weekends to help my dad. Every Friday and Saturday night, our whole family accompanied him to the movie theater so he could get a small respite from the grueling seven-day-a-week work schedule. We usually left the house around midnight and would work until five or six in the morning. We did this every week for a year. My job at the theater was to clean all the bathrooms.

Going to this huge theater on the weekends gave me a taste of what my dad endured every night. Each time I was there, I wept for my dad. The filth and stench of the bathrooms nauseated and disgusted me. I kept thinking: *This is so unfair and humiliating! Why did he have to get laid off? I have to study really hard so I can get a good job and support my parents, so that my dad can leave this miserable place!* I also imagined how isolated and lonely my dad must have felt—being there and cleaning this massive theater by himself, while I and most other people were asleep in our warm, comfortable beds. These thoughts made me angry and sad about the unfairness of the situation, for his losses and sacrifices. Night after night, he was mopping up sticky soft drinks, cleaning up stale popcorn, scraping off gum from the seats, cleaning grimy bathrooms, and picking up people's garbage.

I offered to quit school and work full time so I could help my parents out financially. Perhaps it would help my dad look for another job. But my parents would have no part of it. "You must finish your education!" they insisted.

This experience gave me the drive to continue to excel in school. I swore that my dad's hard work would not be in vain, that I would do everything in my power to succeed academically and professionally.

This was another of the gifts of adversity. Dad taught me to appreciate all the opportunities I'd been given. He worked at the theaters so I could pursue my dreams. To this day, when I think of him toiling away at the theater every night, my eyes still fill with tears. At the same time, I know that *he was proud* to be able to provide for his family. He wouldn't have wanted it any other way.

⸎

During the time my dad worked at the theater, I continued to go to school full time at UC Berkeley while working part time at VYDC in San Francisco. By then I had been promoted twice; I was working as a project coordinator and supervising other staff members. I also continued to see clients on a regular basis, in which I was supervised by Dr. Bart Aoki, a clinical psychologist. He urged me to consider getting my PhD in clinical psychology so I could become a psychologist.

At the same time, I also worked as a research assistant at UC Berkeley on a study that examined teachers' expectations and their effects on children's performance in school. This study included multiple sites in San Francisco. My job was to interview the Vietnamese students and their parents, as well as the teachers in the various schools. The experience made me appreciate the value of research and how it can inform interventions and positively influence people's lives.

As I considered whether to pursue a PhD in psychology, I thought it would be helpful to get additional clinical experience. I took a leave of absence during the fall semester of my fourth year at Berkeley, in 1988, to do an internship in an in-patient unit at San Francisco General Hospital. The work consisted of seeing patients who had major mental illnesses such as schizophrenia, bipolar disorder, and major depression.

The unit director, Dr. Evelyn Lee, took me under her wing and gave me a comprehensive and rich learning experience. She was the first Asian female psychologist I had ever met who was also in a position of power. Her intelligence, warmth, sense of humor, and passion for her work made her an ideal role model and mentor. She encouraged me to get my doctorate in clinical psychology, emphasizing that there was a shortage of Asian female psychologists. As I immersed myself in this internship, I also continued to work at VYDC as a project coordinator and at UC Berkeley as a research assistant.

One month into my internship, Dr. Lee told me I should get more research experience in preparation for graduate school. In particular, she emphasized that it was important to join a team that would allow me to do data collection and analysis and to co-author an academic paper.

Dr. Lee introduced me to Dr. Ladson Hinton, a fourth-year psychiatry resident at UC San Francisco. He stayed on after his residency as a Robert Wood Johnson Clinical Scholar. Dr. Hinton was the lead investigator of the first study to examine the prevalence of psychiatric disorders among newly arrived Vietnamese refugees in the San Francisco area. He and his team of three other psychiatrists were looking for a research assistant who was fluent in Vietnamese to conduct interviews with research subjects, since he himself was not Vietnamese. I had a panel interview with these four psychiatrists, and they gave me the job, promising me the opportunity to work on all phases of the study and to co-author at least one academic paper. The study would take place at the Refugee Clinic, across the street from San Francisco General Hospital.

In November, I began my research work at the Refugee Clinic. I returned to UC Berkeley in the spring as a full-time student while also maintaining my job at VYDC. The first phase of the Vietnamese refugee study involved interviewing newly arrived subjects and screening them for various psychiatric disorders. These interviews revealed that some of the participants suffered from major depression, anxiety, and post-traumatic stress disorder. Most of them had had traumatic experiences in Vietnamese reeducation camps or during their escape out of Vietnam. In response, Dr. Hinton and I collaborated as co-therapists to treat these clients. In the meantime, I also continued to do data collection by interviewing the remaining new arrivals, until we reached our targeted goal of 201 subjects.

My work on this research team lasted eighteen months. Through that time, I had the opportunity to collect data, do data entry and analysis, and co-author three peer-reviewed journal articles. In the world of academics, such papers are a measure of one's productivity and prestige. I was able to accomplish all my research goals on this project with the help and encouragement of Dr. Hinton.

Little did I know at the time that meeting him would turn out to be one of my life's greatest blessings.

CHAPTER 18

New Beginnings

On May 22nd, 1990, I received my BA in psychology, with honors, from UC Berkeley. My dad and siblings came to the graduation, which was held at the Greek Theatre. My mom couldn't attend because she had to work. When I reunited with my family and friends, the first thing I noticed was my dad's big grin as he beamed with pride. He hugged me and told me he was proud of me. "You are the first person in our family to graduate from college. You made this one of the happiest days of my life!"

I thanked him for all the sacrifices he and my mom had made to make this day possible. I thought about our escape from Vietnam and the years my parents had worked at manual-labor jobs to make ends meet. My dad was due to leave in a few hours to work at the multiplex theater.

As we walked back to my apartment, my dad told me he was looking forward to the day when I would get my doctorate in psychology. (By then, I knew that I wanted to go to graduate school.) "I want to be the person to put on your hood," he said, "when you get your PhD in clinical psychology."

The doctoral hood is a long, ornate piece of cloth that's placed onto the graduate at the commencement ceremony. It's worn over the graduation gown and hangs from the neck down one's back. My dad was referring to the part of the ceremony he'd noticed that day, where the various PhD recipients had each chosen a specific person (spouse, parent, mentor) to hood them at the graduation. Though I noted my dad's request at the time, I didn't give it much thought. Earning a PhD seemed like a long shot—I didn't even know if I'd be able to get into a doctoral program in clinical psychology, given how competitive they are. And even if I did, it would take at least five years before I would get my PhD. On top of that, I was taking a gap year to continue my work at VYDC and apply to graduate school.

With Dad and Kathy on my graduation from UC Berkeley, in 1990.

Two weeks after graduation was my last day on the research team at the refugee clinic. I said goodbye to the staff and thanked everyone for their kindness. Then I walked into Dr. Hinton's office to thank him for giving me the opportunity to work on the team.

"You've done a great job here," he replied, smiling. "Can I take you out to dinner to celebrate your graduation?"

It was decided that he'd pick me up at six the following Saturday for dinner.

On June 6th, just two hours before my dinner with Dr. Hinton, water started streaming down from the ceiling of my apartment. I rushed upstairs to where my landlady, Mrs. Fong, lived, and rang the doorbell. She was a Chinese woman in her eighties who had memory problems and was hard of hearing. It took Mrs. Fong quite a while to come to the door. When she finally opened it, she looked like she had just woken up from a nap. She was yelling, "Water, water, water!"

I stepped into her living room—and into several inches of water. I could hear water gushing from the kitchen sink. I quickly ran to turn off the faucet, which was on full blast, and began to help Mrs. Fong mop up the water. While we mopped and she yelled at herself for being careless, I completely lost track of time. By the time I finally looked at the clock, it was already 5:30.

Frazzled, I ran downstairs to take a shower, and I was still getting ready when Dr. Hinton rang the doorbell. I let him in, saying I needed another couple of minutes. Suddenly, he pulled a dozen red roses from behind his back and presented them to me. Then he planted a quick kiss on my lips and said, "Just thought I'd break the ice."

I was shocked speechless and turned to walk away from him.

"Oh my gosh, I'm so sorry!" he said quickly. "I can see I've offended you. I shouldn't have done that. Please forgive me and let me explain."

Dr. Hinton revealed that he had developed feelings for me over the past year but "didn't want to do anything until the research project was over." Now that we were no longer working together, he wanted to know if I'd be interested in dating him. Then he apologized again for the kiss, confessing it was "a stupid idea" suggested by one of his male friends.

"It's uncharacteristic of me to do something like this," he explained. "I wish I hadn't done it."

I was quiet at first, which made him even more nervous. I could see the beads of perspiration on his forehead and his upper lip as he looked at me intently. But finally I spoke. "I've been dreaming about this."

"What?" he exclaimed.

Then it was my turn to explain. "Yes," I smiled. Over the past several months, I'd had multiple dreams about Ladson, about us. In one of the dreams, we sat silently next to each other, yet there was a feeling of affection and warmth between us. In other dreams, he had his arm around me, or we were holding hands as we sat next to each other. I always woke up from these dreams feeling confused and thinking they were really bizarre.

Back then, I didn't fully appreciate the power of the unconscious or intuition. But my unconscious must have picked up Ladson's feelings and communicated them to me through my dreams. On a conscious level, however, I was totally clueless about any romantic feelings he might have had for me, and vice versa.

In our work together, I had seen that Ladson was a gentle, humble, kind, steady, and intelligent person who thought deeply about things. In these ways, he reminded me of my dad. When we worked as co-therapists, I was impressed by his empathy, thoughtfulness, and skill. These qualities were expressed in his interactions with our clients as well as when we debriefed after the sessions. During the time we worked together, I'd gotten to know Ladson and sensed that he was a good, solid person. But that was as far as it went.

After my relationship with the priest ended, I'd had no interest in dating anyone. I totally immersed myself in work and school. I'd been told by my girlfriends at the time that I seemed to purposely and consistently ignore any signs men sent my way about their interest in me. The experience with Father D had distorted my view of what it meant to be in a relationship, emphasizing only how harmful they can be. So having a boyfriend wasn't even on my radar. In light of my history of abuse, I'm grateful that Ladson did not divulge his romantic feelings towards me until my work on the research project was over.

Ladson and I began dating after that. The fact that he wasn't Vietnamese but respected and was interested in Vietnamese language, culture, and food intrigued me. My nuclear and extended family all embraced him because he was humble, kind, funny, and ate everything they offered him.

My parents' initial struggles with their own parents over their relationship made them very understanding. My parents strongly believed that love knows no boundaries—people should be able to love whoever they want, regardless of religion or race.

I think of the evolution and progression of relationships in terms of seasons. When Ladson and I began dating, we entered the spring of our partnership. Things between us felt fun, easy, and exciting. The process of getting to know each other felt intoxicating and exhilarating. The more we talked and spent time with each other, the clearer it became that we were a good match. We were both oldest siblings, and we shared similar values in our appreciation for good food and closeness to our families, as well as our interests in cross-cultural psychology, research, therapy, and enjoyment of travel and the arts. We both loved reading and discovered that we owned a number of the same books. To me it was a good sign that we were compatible.

In February 1991, after dating for eight months, Ladson and I took a weeklong trip to the Sea Ranch, a beautiful coastal area of California bounded by rugged beaches to the west and vast forested land to the east. This place had special meaning for us, since each of us had gone there as children on vacation with our respective families. That week we hiked, walked on the beach, read poetry, talked for hours about various topics, and watched classic movies on TV.

We harvested mussels off the rocks and cooked them immediately after we got back to our rental house. Everything about the vacation seemed to be going splendidly—until we got into our first big argument one night after dinner.

Ladson was due to leave in about a week for Taiwan and China to teach a course on research methods. He'd be away for four months. We talked about my taking some time off from work to join him in China for a vacation in mid-June. During the conversation, he was pushing for me to take a longer vacation. Things heated up. We were diametrically opposed in our positions on the matter. After a while, I announced that I was done arguing and needed a break from the conversation.

Then Ladson blurted out, "Can you imagine being married to such a stubborn man?"

What? I thought. *Married?*

"What the heck! Are you proposing to me right now?"

"Yes," he said, as his expression went from a grimace to a smile.

Needless to say, his unconventional proposal ended our impasse. I said yes.

The day before he proposed, Ladson had found out that he'd been accepted into Harvard's Department of Social Medicine for a postdoctoral fellowship in medical anthropology. It would begin in the fall, after he returned from the trip to Asia. I, on the other hand, was still awaiting word from the clinical psychology programs I'd applied to. So while we were excited about our engagement, it was not clear whether we'd end up in the same city. I was open to the idea of a long-distance relationship, but Ladson strongly opposed it.

———⊗⊗⊗———

Ladson left the following week to teach his class. In those days, even email was a rarity, and forget about FaceTime, Skype, or cell phones. And phone calls to Asia were very expensive. We wrote letters to each other and had a weekly ten-minute phone conversation at midnight my time.

While Ladson was away, I began hearing from the doctoral programs I'd applied to, and I got multiple interviews. One of them was with Boston University, in early March. In May, I was informed that I was admitted into their PhD program in clinical psychology. I also received a scholarship from the American Psychological Association that would pay for my entire graduate education. It was a huge relief to know that Ladson and I would be able to live in the same city and wouldn't be saddled with huge student debts.

Early in June of 1991, I joined Ladson in Beijing, and we spent several weeks exploring that city, as well as Kunming and Guilin. The beauty and history of these places were amazing. Because Ladson was proficient in Mandarin, we were able to travel on our own without a tour group or a guide. People stared at us continuously as we toured the Imperial City in Beijing, as if an Asian woman with a White man were one of the exhibits.

The most memorable thing about our trip to China was that whenever Ladson would begin speaking Mandarin, swarms of people would surround us. They were puzzled about why he was White and spoke Mandarin, while I looked Chinese but didn't speak the language. He was my translator. Each time, Ladson had to explain that I wasn't Chinese, I was Vietnamese.

"Oh, Vietnamese—she's the same as Chinese," they responded. "The Chinese ruled over Vietnam for many years, so she's basically Chinese. But she must learn how to speak Mandarin like you!"

We were both amused by our interactions with the Chinese people and glad that his job as my translator was short lived. After thirteen days, we headed home to prepare for our engagement party.

We had our engagement ceremony on August 11th, 1991.

In Vietnamese culture, the engagement ritual consists of the groom's family coming to the bride's parents' home to ask for her hand in marriage and presenting them with gifts such as wine and food. Since Ladson and his family were unfamiliar with these rituals, my family and I prepared all the gifts so that all they had to do was bring them on the designated day.

Ladson's parents flew down from Seattle for the ceremony, and everything turned out beautifully. They presented the gifts, my parents accepted their request for Ladson and me to marry, and then we shared a traditional Vietnamese meal together.

Our parents got along well despite the ethnic and cultural differences. My dad enjoyed speaking French with Ladson's father, and our mothers bonded over raising children.

Ladson is the oldest of three sons. His middle brother is also a psychiatrist, and his youngest brother is a cultural anthropologist. Ladson's parents are of English, Irish, and Native American ancestry descent. Ladson's father, Dr. Walter Ladson Hinton III, is a Jungian psychoanalyst; his mother was a stay-at-home mom. His parents were born and raised in Arkansas, moved to Palo Alto, California, in the 1970s, and then relocated to Seattle in 1990.

Shortly after the ceremony Ladson and I left for Boston, and took our time driving cross-country. We were both in awe of the beauty of our great nation. It was especially interesting to see the differences in the landscape and the local cultures of each city we passed through.

A lot of people stared at us as we drove through the Midwest, probably because people there seldom saw interracial couples. This experience made us realize that our relationship was perceived differently in different parts of the country.

After four weeks, we arrived in Boston. We rented a two-bedroom, one-bath Victorian condo with a fireplace. It was close to public transportation (the T), which allowed easy access to my school and Ladson's work. I began my PhD program at Boston University, and Ladson started his postdoctoral fellowship at Harvard in medical anthropology.

It was a culture shock to go from the San Francisco Bay Area to Boston. Although many people told me that Boston was the San Francisco of Massachusetts, I was struck by the enormous differences. In general, I found the people in Boston to be more reserved and formal, but generally in a nice way. Maybe it was because Boston was so much older than San Francisco. Founded in 1630, it had centuries of history and social hierarchy based on how long your family had been there, in contrast to San Francisco's younger, more diverse and tolerant society.

Our first winter there was brutal. I was never able to stay warm enough, even though I wore three layers under a down jacket. The nor'easter storms were beautiful and magical—until we had to shovel our sidewalk and dig our car out of the snow. Parking was a bear. Sometimes we had to circle for thirty minutes before we could find a space on the street. The black ice also made walking treacherous, resulting in multiple falls. Our fireplace was a real lifesaver during those cold winter nights.

On one of my first rides on the T, I saw two White men in business suits yelling at two elderly Asian women to "stop speaking Chinese." I was so shocked and incensed by the incident that I confronted the men. "Stop it!" I yelled. "How dare you tell these women to stop speaking their language. You should be ashamed of yourself!"

Evidently these men were as shocked by my screaming at them as I was by their disrespect for these women. I probably shattered their stereotype of the timid and deferential Asian woman. In any case, they stopped harassing the women the moment I intervened. What struck me about the incident was that none of the other bystanders responded in any way. It was as if this was business as usual.

Ladson and I also encountered racism personally when we looked for rentals. On two separate occasions, Ladson went to look at apartments, signed the lease, and put down the deposits. But when I came with him to look at the places, the landlords announced that the apartments were no longer available. These unpleasant racial experiences, as well as the extent of the segregation I observed in the various ethnic neighborhoods of Boston—Irish, African American, Italian—made me question whether we'd made a mistake by moving to Boston. At the same time, I loved the gorgeous fall foliage and the abundant exposure to American history.

During my first several months in Boston, I connected with my classmates and got good grades in all my classes, but I clashed with some of my male professors. When I'd raise my hand to respond to questions they had posed, they would point to me. "What does this assertive liberal Asian Californian have to tell us?"

These incidents left me feeling stigmatized and made me question whether I belonged in this school. In particular, I found my psychoanalytic theory class excruciating to sit through. In this course, we read most of Sigmund Freud's twenty-four–volume Complete Psychological Works. For the first time, I was exposed to concepts such as penis envy and the Oedipal complex. According to Freud, penis envy is a stage in girls' psychosexual development when they experience anxiety and envy upon figuring out that they don't have a penis. This realization is supposed to cause them to move from being attached to their mother to competing with their mother for their father's attention and affection. Similarly, the Oedipal complex is a child's supposed unconscious sexual desire for the opposite-sex parent and hatred for the same-sex parent.

I couldn't relate to anything I was reading in this class. It was like a different language. I was also frustrated by the inherently sexist, classist, misogynistic, homophobic, and Euro-centric views expressed in Freud's writings. I questioned how any of these theories applied to clinical work, especially with clients of color, those who weren't from the upper-middle class, those who didn't identify as being heterosexual, or those with major mental illnesses such as schizophrenia. As hard as I'd tried, I couldn't see for the life of me how these psychoanalytic theories applied to my work with refugees in San Francisco or those who were on the in-patient units. Not surprisingly, my professor didn't appreciate or respond well to my various inquiries.

These clashes with some of my professors continued for several months, eventually beginning to affect my mood. I felt discouraged and seriously considered leaving the program. Then I recalled my dad's request to hood me at my PhD graduation. I changed my attitude and decided that I wouldn't quit. I would persevere, immerse myself in every course, and take in all that my professors had to offer. I decided that if I wanted to question what I was learning, I had to first master the material. From that point on, I found a new appreciation for my professors and what I was learning.

In this I was helped by, for the first time, having the luxury of just going to school and not juggling several jobs at the same time. This first year of graduate school turned out to be one of the most growth-enhancing years of my life.

At the same time, Ladson and I (well, mostly I) were also planning a wedding across the country. There were many issues to sift through, since we wanted to integrate our two cultures into the Catholic mass, and planned a sit-down banquet for 350 guests. The mass would be held at my church in Concord, and the meal at a Chinese restaurant in Oakland.

On a beautiful summer day in 1992, Ladson and I got married. We had a half-mass that integrated a Vietnamese reading and was celebrated by a Vietnamese and an American priest. I wore my white American wedding dress at the mass, and later changed into a long red *ao dai* for the banquet. It's customary for Vietnamese brides to wear red, since it signifies good luck.

Ladson and me on our wedding day in 1992, with my parents.

The dinner included a ten-course meal and was followed by music and dancing. We adhered to the Vietnamese tradition of going to all the tables accompanied by our parents to greet and thank our guests. At each table, friends and families bestowed their best wishes for happiness upon us, and then presented us with envelopes filled with money. This ritual allows the bride and groom to not incur debt from the wedding. Ladson announced on that day that our future children would all have Vietnamese weddings.

While it was one of the happiest days of my life, an invisible cloud still loomed over me. I couldn't fully enjoy the day because I was keeping a dark secret from Ladson. And as a result, I was harboring deep feelings of shame and guilt. I wished I had the courage to tell him the secret I was hiding, but I was too terrified of what it might do to our relationship.

CHAPTER 19

Seasons of a Marriage

In the fall of 1992, I began my second year of graduate school. I took a full course load while completing a twenty-hour-per-week clinical practicum at an outpatient community mental health center that served ethnically diverse, low-income clients with major mental illnesses. In my graduate program, all students were also strongly encouraged to engage in our own therapy. (I agree that therapists are more able to help clients if they've done their own psychological work.) So I entered individual therapy for the second time that fall and worked extensively on my childhood sexual trauma and the problems that were emerging in my relationship with Ladson.

For the first time, eleven years after the abuse began and almost five years after it ended, I began to talk about what *really* happened to me. I discussed in detail with my therapist, Dr. K, how Father D had come into my life, the summer road trip where I was basically held hostage, how I was threatened to keep the abuse a secret, the duration and severity of the abuse, the depth of the betrayal to me and my family, how I managed to get away, and the harm the abuse had caused me. When I entered therapy this time, I had full blown post-traumatic stress disorder. Nightmares of Father D returned with a vengeance, plaguing me multiple times a week and disrupting my sleep. This in turn caused difficulties in my attention, concentration, and memory. I also became more depressed and had bouts of wanting to end my life.

My therapy focused initially on decreasing my depression, PTSD, and suicidal thoughts. As these issues subsided, my work progressed into acknowledging and mourning what the perpetrator stole from me: my sense of innocence, my childhood, my trust in priests and the Catholic Church, the purity of a first kiss, the freedom to choose in all matters that pertained to my relationship with boys my age— including my readiness for physical intimacy at various stages—and my sense of self.

I struggled with immense feelings of self-blame and shame. With Dr. K's help, I came to realize that the abuse was not my fault and I was not responsible for any of it. For the first time, I recognized that I was a child when Father D manipulated, threatened, and took advantage of me. Dr. K also laid out in detail the myriad ways that Father D's behaviors were unethical and criminal. With greater understanding and knowledge, I began to heal, developed more self-compassion, and faced the reality of how pervasively the abuse had affected me. At the same time, I learned that the abuse did not define who I was as a person; it was something that happened to me. These realizations gradually helped me to decrease my feelings of shame, guilt, and sense of responsibility for the abuse.

About six months into my therapy, Dr. K brought up the idea of telling Ladson about my abuse. I balked at first. I was still too fearful of what it might do to our marriage. I didn't know whether we would be able to deal with it as a couple. I was concerned that he might perceive me as being "damaged," blame me for what happened, or feel betrayed and angry that I didn't tell him about the abuse before we got married. I was convinced that revealing the secret to Ladson would destroy our marriage, and that terrified me.

Dr. K persisted and helped me to work through my fears. We discussed the benefits of complete honesty with Ladson, and the relief I would gain from relinquishing the secret. Keeping the truth from Ladson became more painful for me with each passing day. I felt that I was being dishonest. Ladson deserved to know the whole truth about me and my history. After months of mulling things over and talking through all my apprehensions with Dr. K, I was ready to take the plunge, reveal everything to Ladson, and let the chips fall where they may.

One weekend morning in the fall of 1993, after we'd eaten our breakfast at home, I told Ladson I needed to talk to him about something important. With great trepidation, I told Ladson what had happened with Father D. I wept as I shared in detail the camping trip from hell, how the abuse continued throughout high school and into college, and how I finally managed to break away from Father D. While I felt terrified, raw, and exposed, it was also utterly liberating to finally tell Ladson the whole truth about what had happened.

The telling took several hours. Ladson listened patiently, held my hand, comforted me, and helped me get through it. His warmth, compassion, and deep listening made it safe to disclose everything. It was a sacred, healing, and powerful experience to finally break free from the silence and secrecy. I felt immense relief and an incredible sense of lightness after it was all over. Then we held each other and cried.

I wept from the immense relief of being able to reveal the secret to Ladson, and he cried for the pain and suffering I'd endured through the years. He told me how sorry he was for what Father D did to me and expressed his rage towards the man.

"I wish I could find the bastard and kill him!"

At the same time, Ladson emphasized that he didn't see me in a different light, that I was still his wife, the woman he fell in love with, and he would stay by my side to help me through everything and anything. Together we'd be able weather this storm.

"Are you mad?" I asked him. "Do you feel betrayed that I didn't tell you this before we got married?"

He thought for a moment. I could tell he was choosing his words carefully.

"I wish you would've told me so you didn't have to carry the secret, but it wouldn't have changed how I felt about you or my desire to marry you. If anything, I have more respect for you now, knowing everything you've been through."

His compassionate response was a turning point for me. From that day forward, I no longer felt alone on my journey of healing. With him by my side, I was hopeful that I'd be able to heal from my sexual trauma and we would indeed be able to weather this storm together.

I was relieved that Ladson didn't want to leave me after finding out the truth about my abuse, especially because we had begun having problems several months after we got married. The season of our marriage had changed drastically then, and not for the better. Our blissful springtime courtship, which evolved into the summer dream wedding, quickly ended. The autumn season of our marriage descended upon us, and multiple difficulties emerged.

We argued incessantly, about everything under the sun. We had different ideas about how to keep our apartment clean, for instance. I was neat and meticulous about doing my chores, while Ladson tended to be more relaxed about cleanliness and less consistent about cleaning up on a regular basis. We encountered other typical challenges newly married couples face. Also, my relationship with Ladson's mother was complicated, and we struggled to navigate that.

Ladson and I are both strong-willed, oldest children, and our gender, ethnic, and cultural differences played a role in polarizing and escalating us in our discussions with each other. We did not yet know how to differentiate from our families-of-origin to form our own rituals and establish a united front. When we fought we didn't communicate well, by listening to each other's perspective. Instead we dug in our heels and became judgmental or condescending or raised our voices. We didn't know how to disagree in a civil manner.

Away from home we were both experiencing a lot of stress in our academic pursuits. Ladson was working hard to prove himself professionally at Harvard, while I was juggling a full course load and seeing clients—as well as dealing with symptoms of depression and PTSD.

After over a year of this and a few months after I told Ladson about my abuse, we realized we had to get professional help. We entered couple's therapy at the beginning of 1994, while I continued to work on my own therapy with Dr. K. Our entry into couple's therapy marked the dark and difficult winter season of our marriage. We were never physically violent with each other, but we were both unhappy in the relationship and wondered whether we had made a mistake by choosing each other. In spite of our misgivings, we promised each other that we'd put in our best efforts to save the marriage. We pledged to be truthful, faithful, and accept the final outcome if one of us decided to end the relationship. If we parted ways, it would be done in the spirit of mutual respect and loving-kindness, knowing that we both tried our best.

With heavy hearts and great determination, Ladson and I hunkered down and got to work on our marriage. We were willing to do whatever it took to change our unhealthy dynamics while staying true to who we were as individuals. The work was slow, long, and grueling. Small steps forward were frequently followed by multiple steps back. My sense of despondency and pessimism for the survival of our marriage manifested in several repetitive dreams. In one of them, Ladson and I were stranded on a small wooden boat, bobbing in a rough sea amid a ferocious rainstorm. The heavy rain and winds hammered us as we struggled to find our way back to the safety of shore.

Another nightmare often occurred after we got into a heated argument. It was the same one I'd had on the first night after Father D assaulted me on the camping trip, where I was chased down and assaulted. But now, the face of the man sometimes morphed into Ladson's. These scary dreams left me feeling enraged at Father D and wondering whether I'd ever be truly free of him. I hated that he was still intruding by tormenting me in my sleep and wreaking havoc in my relationship with Ladson.

From the nightmares, it was obvious that whenever Ladson and I fought, I began to think of Ladson as Father D. This dynamic made it hard for me to trust Ladson, confide in him, or lean on him for support. During these times, I coped by becoming ultra-independent (a childhood coping mechanism), withdrawing into myself, and shutting Ladson out. I became physically and emotionally distant, and occasionally took off on my own for hours at a time, sometimes in the middle of the night. I would buy cigarettes at a convenience store down the street, and then while smoking I'd walk for miles to dark, secluded, unsafe parks or areas of town without telling Ladson where I was or when I'd be returning (remember, this was before most people had even heard of mobile phones). These runaways lasted up to several hours.

Other times, I became suicidal and contemplated various ways to end my life. I researched the most effective way to cut my wrist to get the job done and which over-the-counter medications provided the swiftest death.

Thankfully I never followed through on any of these plans. While I desperately wanted the pain to end, I didn't want to die. I loved Ladson, my friends, and family and didn't want to leave them or burden them with the heartache of my suicide. In couple's therapy, we began by focusing on issues of safety. Dr. M, our couple's therapist, helped me make an agreement with Ladson. I promised not to harm myself, to let Ladson know if I felt suicidal, and not walk out of the house in the middle of the night. If I needed to leave, I had to let Ladson know where I was going—and it had to be a safe place—and when I'd be returning.

Then we focused on learning ways to communicate more effectively, calmly, and respectfully. We refrained from discussing sensitive topics late at night, using generalizations such as "always" or "never," engaging in all-or-nothing thinking, and using language that was provocative and hurtful. Instead, we used mindfulness techniques to cultivate skills of deep listening, empathy, and compassion, and tried to see things from the other person's perspective.

One of the techniques we practiced was called the rock exercise. We took turns speaking while holding a stone. The person holding the stone spoke while the other person listened. The listener was silent, concentrating on hearing with an open heart, while the person who was speaking tried to do so calmly, honestly, and respectfully. We also practiced affect-regulation techniques to control our negative emotions so that we could disagree without escalating. These tools helped us express our differences more effectively, negotiate household chores, and minimize our feelings of resentment and anger. We also explored how various family-of-origin patterns affected our worldviews, shaped our expectations for the marriage, and influenced the way we behaved towards each other.

These insights enabled us to form a more united front in our interactions with our respective families and allowed us to create our own customs, rituals, and boundaries as a couple. Most importantly, we educated ourselves on how my past traumas, especially the sexual trauma, impacted our relationship in the here and now. We read books about trauma and learned techniques to recognize and manage the triggers as they arose.

In one of our sessions, about a year into the couple's therapy, Ladson broke down and cried as he talked about how excruciatingly painful it was for him to hear me scream and cry out at night during my bad dreams. These nightmares plagued me on most nights during the first several years of our marriage. My heart swelled with deep compassion for Ladson when I heard and saw his distress. In that moment, I recognized how hard it must have been for him to be married to a trauma survivor. He'd had to witness how the sexual abuse affected me, deal with the turmoil that it caused in our lives, and be strong for me while trying to support me emotionally. Who was supporting and being strong for him?

Seeing how Ladson also suffered made me realize that both of us were victims of Father D's abuse. I gained a deeper love and appreciation for Ladson, for his kindness, patience, and willingness to support me—and for not giving up on us. This incident played a pivotal role in transforming my perception of Ladson and of our marriage. For the first time, I saw that we were true partners on my journey of healing, and the trauma was our foe. We had to work together as a team to fight this enemy or it would destroy us.

After persevering through three arduous years of couple's therapy, Ladson and I emerged from the winter of our marriage with more hope, knowledge, and tools to navigate our differences and challenges. The process of therapy deepened our bond, made us stronger, and gave us a deeper appreciation for one another.

I'm deeply thankful to Ladson for being my rock and my companion on my journey of healing, and for being my partner for all seasons.

As you can see from my experience with Ladson, trauma affects both the survivor and his or her partner. Because of this, it's essential for couples who face trauma-related difficulties to get treatment. It's most helpful to find a therapist who has expertise treating trauma. As a therapist who has spent over twenty years working with couples who suffer from trauma-related issues, I want to emphasize that trauma is a formidable foe. You need a skilled therapist to help you battle its effects together.

At the same time, know that the fight against trauma can certainly be won. With love, determination, and perseverance, you and your partner can transform your experience from being victims of trauma to becoming allied warriors on the path of healing. You will emerge from therapy feeling stronger, closer, and more able to deal with the trauma, as well as other life challenges.

One of the greatest gifts that can emerge from working through our own trauma is a deep sense of gratitude. Recognizing that we have the tenacity and courage to do the hard work of healing engenders in us a sense of gratitude towards ourselves, for our own resilience and strength, as well as towards others who have accompanied us on our journey of healing.

In spite of the turbulence in my marriage and my struggles to heal from the trauma, I managed to get through five years of graduate school. During these years, I maintained good grades, got my master's degree in clinical psychology, taught several undergraduate classes, worked as a teaching assistant, served on the admissions committee for the PhD clinical psychology program, worked as a therapist twenty hours a week, volunteered at a domestic violence shelter, served as a board member and then co-president of the board of directors for an agency that provided services to domestic violence survivors, passed my comprehensive exams, and defended my dissertation.

My dissertation was the first study to examine the issue of domestic violence among Vietnamese refugee women in America. Within a year, I interviewed sixty-five women, analyzed the data, and defended my dissertation. My study revealed that Vietnamese women had higher rates of lifetime physical abuse and suffered more severe acts of abuse compared to women in the general U.S. population. It also showed that the abused women in the study had higher rates of depression and PTSD, were less educated, held more traditional attitudes about gender roles, and had partners who drank and were less satisfied with their jobs compared to the non-abused women.

I was amazed by the willingness of the abused women to talk about their experiences of domestic violence. Many of them emphasized that it was helpful and liberating to talk to a Vietnamese female psychologist about their "family secret." It helped them to feel understood and less alone. I provided these women with resources for therapy and other services in case they wanted additional support. Not surprisingly, the Vietnamese women who embraced more traditional gender roles and cultural beliefs were less likely to want therapy or to obtain other services for domestic violence, since it would require them to reveal their abuse.

After defending my dissertation, in 1996, I went on to do my internship at Harvard Medical School at the Massachusetts Mental Health Center. I worked with adults and children and received amazing training and supervision. One of my clinical supervisors was Dr. Mariko Sakurai, a Japanese American psychologist. In one of our supervision sessions, we somehow got onto the topic of my being a Vietnamese refugee. Dr. Sakurai stopped in her tracks, leaned in, looked me in the eye, and said, "You have to write a book about your escape!"

I was touched by her enthusiasm and intrigued by the idea of writing a book. But it was the last thing on my mind. I was working sixty hours a week and barely had enough time to sleep or spend quality time with Ladson. I was eager to complete my stimulating, yet grueling, internship year so I could begin my career as a psychologist and start a family.

Dr. Sakurai often reiterated the importance of "writing the book." At the end of my internship, when I said goodbye to her, she hugged me and reminded me again to someday find the time to write a book about my escape.

On May 18th, 1997, I received my PhD in clinical psychology from Boston University (BU). My entire family flew out for the event.

At my graduation from Boston University in 1997,
with my siblings: Jane, Kathy, me, Betty, and Robbie.

Since BU required that the dissertation advisor hood the graduate at the commencement, I asked my dad to do the honor of hooding me at home before we headed out for the graduation ceremony. The moment he placed the hood onto me, I was overcome with emotion. I remembered our conversation seven years earlier, when I graduated from UC Berkeley. It was my dad's fervent desire to hood me that provided me with the will and determination to push through the hard times during graduate school and got me to the finish line.

With dad at my graduation from BU. Knowing that it was his dream to hood me on this special day inspired me to persevere through grad school and make it to the finish line.

Unbeknownst to me, when I walked across the stage to receive my doctoral diploma that day, I became the first Vietnamese woman to receive a PhD in clinical psychology in America.

———

Two months after my graduation, in July 1997, I returned to Vietnam for the first time, accompanied by Ladson, my parents, and my sister Jane. Over twenty-two years had passed since our harrowing escape. The trip began with a visit to North Vietnam, where we visited my mom's relatives—her paternal uncle and maternal aunts and cousins.

My extended family was impressed by Ladson's command of Vietnamese, as well as his deep appreciation and respect for our culture. Ladson had taken Vietnamese language classes at Harvard for two years before embarking on our trip, and we'd practiced speaking Vietnamese every night. We also paid homage to my mom's ancestors by visiting them at the Ho ancestral hall and bowing to them with incense sticks. We were surprised to find that this ancestral hall was designated as a historical site by the communist government. Until then, I was unaware that my mom is a distant relative of Ho Chi Minh. My mom's family had kept this fact under wraps, for obvious reasons.

We also visited Nho Quan and Hai Phong, two places where my mom had lived as a young girl and fled from on foot during the war. In Ha Noi, Ladson and I visited various tourist sites. At each point of entry, the gatekeepers assumed that I was Ladson's tour guide, since I spoke Vietnamese to them, and charged me fees that were only a tenth of his.

Then we went south to Saigon to visit my old home and school. Everything looked smaller than I remembered it, but the streets were much more congested with mopeds, bicycles, and cars. Returning to Saigon with my family brought back many fond memories of our happy, simple, comfortable life during my childhood. Our evening strolls to the park and ice cream parlors came back to me. The car ride from my old house to my old school reminded me of when I sat in the back with Betty and my dad, as our chauffeur drove us to school in the mornings. Now my dad was no longer the army major in his shiny black boots and crisply pressed uniform, but a tourist in his old homeland.

Then we headed further south, to Can Tho and Long Xuyen, to visit my dad's siblings, aunts, uncles, and cousins. It was especially moving to see my dad reunited with his brothers and sisters after not seeing them for over two decades. Shortly after our arrival, we traveled to my paternal grandfather's gravesite. My parents, Ladson, my sister Jane, and I kneeled at the foot of my paternal grandfather's grave with incense sticks in our hands and bowed to him in unison. He had died on March 27th, 1993, two years before the U.S. normalized diplomatic relations with Vietnam, which had made it impossible for us to visit my grandfather before his passing or attend his funeral.

This ritual of honoring my paternal grandfather at his gravesite was the main reason we'd returned to Vietnam. For years, my parents—especially my dad—had longed for this day, and it had taken this long for them to save up enough money to make this trip back.

Then I heard my dad ask his father for forgiveness. "I'm sorry that I was not able to fulfill my duties as your son, and care for you in your old age," he said, choking up. "But now I have come to tell you goodbye."

Ladson embraced and comforted me as I cried for my father's feelings of regret and the many lost opportunities due to the consequences of war. At the same time, I felt a deep sense of gratitude and closure. Being in Vietnam with my family helped me to heal from the wounds of my escape. It allowed me to appreciate that we all made it out safely and were now back to honor my grandfather.

CHAPTER 20

Gifts of Life

In June of 1998, Ladson and I moved from Boston back to California to be closer to family. By then, I had completed a postdoctoral year of clinical work, was studying for my licensing exam, and was seven months pregnant with our first child. Ladson took an assistant professor position in the UC Davis School of Medicine's psychiatry department, while I got us settled into our new rental home.

Ladson faced considerable work pressures to publish, while also excelling in his research and clinical work, in the hope of being able to make tenure in seven years. This was the reality of the "publish or perish" academic environment.

To add to everything else we had going on, we had purchased a plot of land on a cul-de-sac and were excited to build our new home. I worked with the contractor to make it all happen. It was fun, exciting, and laborious to research all the options for the house design, as well as the paint colors, tile, grout, cabinets, countertops, carpet, appliances ... This was long before home products could be previewed online, so I had to spend hours driving to Home Depot and other stores. My car was filled with samples of paint colors and everything else that went into making a house into a home.

Every evening, Ladson and I drove to the new house to inspect the progress being made on its construction. While we were excited to see that things were going smoothly, our house wouldn't be ready until December, so our daughter would be born before the house was completed.

On a gorgeous fall day of that year, Carina Kimlan was born at 12:54 p.m., weighing seven and a half pounds, with a full head of shiny black hair. We decided to give her a Vietnamese middle name to honor her Vietnamese heritage and to name her after my dad's oldest sister. Ladson was by my side throughout the thirty-six hours of labor and delivery. I will never forget the incredible feelings of exhilaration, love, and warmth I felt when I held Carina in my arms for the first time. She was laid on my bare chest immediately after birth, her huge, bewildered hazel eyes looking into mine, as if she was saying, "Hello world."

Ladson and I were elated and relieved that everything went well, especially because Carina's labor had to be induced. She was a full week past her due date and had begun to show signs of respiratory distress. My doctor didn't want to take any chances and urged us to induce immediately. Thankfully, Carina came out healthy, without any complications. I was in awe of my body and grateful that it had the capacity to carry and then give birth to my precious child.

When Carina was about five weeks old, we gave her a big one-month party in accordance with Vietnamese custom. Over seventy guests came to celebrate her birth, healthy development, and give the traditional gold bracelets and necklaces. The guests were pleasantly surprised when Ladson gave a speech in Vietnamese thanking them for their love and support.

My parents were very helpful after Carina was born. Several times a week they braved the heavy commuter traffic after work (ninety minutes each way) to deliver delicious pots of Vietnamese food, which usually lasted us for several days. This lightened our stress level and was greatly appreciated, since Carina had colic the first several months.

My parents bonded with Carina from the start and spent a lot of time with her. Whenever Ladson went out of town on business trips to give talks or present papers at various conferences or universities, Carina and I would go to stay with my parents, where she was surrounded by love and attention. Ladson and I were also grateful for the free childcare, which allowed us to get away for date nights and occasional overnight trips.

Carina's birth filled my heart with delight. She was an alert, engaging, happy baby. I spoke to her in Vietnamese and sang Vietnamese songs to her. She also enjoyed hearing Ladson sing and play the guitar to her every night after dinner. Having Carina awakened deep feelings of devotion, tenderness, and protectiveness I had never known before.

When Carina was about three months old, I began to have nightmares of Father D again after being free of them for a couple of years. In these bad dreams, he came after Carina and tried to hurt her while I fought him off with knives. I awoke from these dreams feeling exhausted and angry. I couldn't believe that he was still haunting me in my dreams and disrupting my life, even though I hadn't seen him for over ten years. The resurgence of my nightmares and intrusive thoughts about Father D prompted me to enter therapy for the fourth time.

I returned to therapy to get help with the reemergence of my PTSD symptoms and to get support to report him to the authorities. I felt that my nightmares and the resurfacing memories of Father D were communicating my need to protect other children from him. I knew that he was working as a psychologist at the time but didn't know whether he was seeing children in his practice. Regardless, I felt a moral obligation to report him to the police, the California Board of Psychology, and the Catholic Church. I couldn't live with myself if I didn't do everything in my power to protect other potential victims. I wrote a comprehensive letter detailing Father D's abuse of me and sent it to the Church and the Board of Psychology. I also filed a police report.

The Catholic diocese wrote me back a two-sentence letter informing me that it had "no record of a Father D serving as a priest." I surmised from this that he was no longer in the priesthood. I would have preferred no response at all, given its callousness. There was no expression of regret for what had happened to me, nor any offer to provide me with resources for therapy.

I was devastated to learn from the Board of Psychology that the seven-year statute of limitations had passed. This meant that the board couldn't investigate my claim of sexual abuse or revoke Father D's license. Similarly, I was five years too late in filing my report with law enforcement. The abuse ceased to be a crime once I turned eighteen, and the criminal statute of limitations was ten years at the time.

I felt heartbroken that my attempts to protect other potential victims had failed. I wished I had known about the statutes of limitations earlier and been able to make reports before the deadlines. But deep down, I knew that I couldn't have done anything different. My healing required time, and there was nothing I could have done to rush the process. At the end of the day, I had to face the fact that I did the best that I could.

Carina's birth also triggered feelings of protectiveness for my siblings. I needed to find out whether Father D had abused any of them. So ten years after I extricated myself from Father D, I finally talked to my siblings individually to find out the truth. I was devastated to learn that Father D had also violated one of my sisters. I was consumed by feelings of rage, disgust, and grief for days after finding out. For the first time, I had the desire to kill another human being. I fantasized about hunting him down, interrogating him, and torturing him. Thankfully, my meditation practice helped to keep me grounded during this difficult time, and I never acted on these fantasies. Still, I wished I could have done something to protect my sister!

Since finding out about each other's abuse, my sister and I have supported each other to heal from its aftermath. We take solace in knowing that we have liberated ourselves from holding the secret and have each other to lean on. Shortly after finding out about each other's abuse, we sat down with my parents to tell them. They were devastated and felt horribly betrayed by Father D.

My dad wept bitterly. "I want to kill this man!" he said. "He hurt my innocent daughters!"

My sister and I also revealed the abuse to our siblings together. Even though it's been over twenty years since the abuse has come to light, my entire family still struggles from its impact. We've been grappling with our feelings about the Catholic Church, its priests, our faith, and whether we want to continue participating in the Church. Some of my siblings decided to stop attending mass, which has caused my parents great sadness and disappointment over the years. It's infuriating that Father D has gotten away with committing atrocious acts of abuse while my family and I are left to pick up the pieces.

It's important to emphasize that childhood abuse affects not just the survivor but also his or her entire family. As a result, I recommend that all survivors and their family members who have been harmed by issues of childhood abuse get therapy and support to deal with the short and long-term effects of the abuse.

Professional support is especially important if a child was sexually abused and the perpetrator is a family member or had a close relationship with the family. Sometimes finding out about the abuse can cause friction and factions within the family; some family members may not believe the survivor and accuse him or her of lying. The closer the relationship and the more power the perpetrator has within the family, the greater the likelihood that family members will have difficulty believing the survivor and holding the perpetrator responsible for the abuse. When this happens, we need to acknowledge each person's feelings and experience and find compassionate ways to support and educate survivors as well as their family members.

Psychoeducation is crucial and should include information on how the survivor and the family was manipulated and deceived by the perpetrator. Family members should also be educated on how the perpetrator groomed, brainwashed, and threatened the child to conceal the abuse and made the child feel responsible for it.

In over twenty years of work with survivors and their families, I've seen well-meaning family members make comments that retraumatized the survivor. Comments that are most helpful to the survivor include: "I'm so sorry this happened to you." "I wish I could have protected you." "I'm here for you now." "Please let me know how I can support you." "It was not your fault."

Family members should refrain from making any comments that imply that the survivor is at fault for the abuse. Such statements may include: "Why did it take you so long to tell?" "If it was so bad, why didn't you tell anyone at the time?" "You were a willing participant in the relationship." "It happened a long time ago. You need to get over it—bury the past. Don't talk about it anymore."

Please keep in mind that whereas the abuse was a horrible thing that happened to you and your family, revealing the truth can be an opportunity to come together, support each other, and heal from the pain.

My faith means a great deal to me, and there are many things about the Catholic Church that I love and admire, such as its good works with the poor and underprivileged, strong positions on human rights issues, and sacred rituals. However, the Church's complicity and inaction in the sexual abuse crisis, as well as its indifferent and insensitive responses to the victims and their families, have been unacceptable, disgraceful, and painful.

It's unconscionable that the Church has repeatedly chosen to protect the offenders rather than the victims. Until very recently, the Church consistently sided with the abusers by refusing to expose their identities or defrock them. The fact that bishops within the Church protected these pedophiles for decades, by moving them from parish to parish, and knowingly put innocent children at risk, is horrifying. It broke my heart when I learned that three hundred priests in Pennsylvania had abused over a thousand children. What was particularly revolting and chilling about these crimes was the fact that some of the abusing priests gave their victims crucifixes to wear that marked them as targets for abuse by other offending priests. This is just pure evil!

Pope Francis's sexual abuse summit ended on February 24th, 2019, with more platitudes and inaction. Astonishingly, the Church has yet to take a forceful or wide-ranging zero-tolerance policy on the abuse of children, nor has it mandated that all abusers be turned into the police.

As a Catholic and a survivor of priest sexual abuse, I ask the Church, how can you let these disgusting things happen, especially to the children? Why do you keep enabling this atrocious system of abuse? I demand that the Catholic Church take responsibility by publicly exposing the names of *all* offenders, defrocking them, and turning them in to law enforcement.

In the U.S. alone, it's estimated that from 1956 to 2016, 6,846 priests abused as many as 100,000 children (Father Andrew Greeley's partial estimate) and at least 18,565 children (survivors who sent allegations to bishops). Yet, only 848 priests have been defrocked *worldwide* according to the Vatican's report in May of 2014. It's also important to point out that the victims of priest sexual abuse in the Catholic Church have not only been children, but also nuns, seminarians, and adult female parishioners—worldwide.

I urge the Church to give restitution to all survivors and pay therapy bills for the survivors and their family members. The Church also needs to expose the names of all bishops who were complicit in hiding the abuse and hold them accountable. In 2002, it was estimated that two-thirds of sitting bishops kept perpetrating priests in the ministry or moved them to other churches. These bishops need to at least apologize personally to all the victims and their family members for harming them.

Another new Vatican tribunal needs to be formed, with 50 percent of its members consisting of survivors from all walks of life and all countries that were affected by the crisis. The tribunal should make recommendations to the Vatican on how to discipline bishops who abetted the abuse and steps that need to be taken to eliminate the sexual abuse in the Catholic Church entirely. The Vatican should then make every effort to act on the tribunal's proposals.

In 2015, Pope Francis approved a tribunal to be formed to assess the behaviors of bishops who concealed and failed to act in cases of sexual abuse by priests. However, the tribunal was never implemented due to the resistance from the upper echelons of the Church and the Congregation for the Doctrine of the Faith, a 477-year-old organization in Rome that circulates and defends Catholic teachings. The failure to form a tribunal caused at least two members (an abuse survivor and a counselor for abuse victims) of the Pontifical Commission for the Protection of Minors to resign, citing inaction, lack of transparency, and resistance from the bishops and the Church.

I also urge Pope Francis to investigate and revamp all systems within the Church that cause, contribute to, or are complicit in sustaining the sexual abuse problem. This needs to include a scrutiny of the seminary, which has been reported to inflict and cultivate multiple generations of sexual abuse. The bogus claim that the sexual abuse crisis is due to problems related to homosexuality is pure nonsense, a pathetic attempt to avoid responsibility and deny the enormity of the problem. The Church must be willing to at least examine how its inaction in the sexual abuse crisis is related to power, the abuse of power, its disavowal of responsibility, and an unwillingness to take strong action against its own.

On February 25th, 2019, Pope Francis's top financial advisor, Cardinal George Pell, was convicted of child sexual abuse. A week before that, U.S. Cardinal Theodore McCarrick was defrocked for committing sex crimes against minors and adults. But in March that same year, Pope Francis rejected the resignation of French Cardinal Philippe Barbarin, who was convicted and sentenced for failing to report sex abuse by a priest under his authority.

I hope and pray that the Catholic Church will find the courage and the will to examine itself and take action to rectify its profound failures in dealing with the sexual abuse crisis. My faith in God, Jesus, and Mother Mary remains unshaken; I did not let the perpetrator take that away from me. The people I've lost faith in are the leaders of the Catholic Church, for their failure to act and their callous responses to the victims and their families. The Church has an enormous amount of work to do before it can regain the trust of its flock.

As a society, we also need to reexamine our laws regarding statutes of limitations on reporting and prosecuting rape, incest, and physical and sexual abuse. The current laws reflect a woeful ignorance of what abuse survivors go through, the time that it takes them to heal from their abuse, and the obstacles survivors face in reporting such crimes. Given that this is the case, it is imperative that we eliminate time limits for reporting such atrocities. Legal action for physical and sexual abuse should be given the same latitude as homicides, for which there is no time limit for reporting or prosecuting the crime.

It's important to recognize that childhood abuse is an inhumane act of violence against an innocent and defenseless human being. Its impact is far-ranging and can impair a survivor's sense of self, as well as his or her development and functioning for many decades.

It's important to keep in mind, moreover, that many survivors of abuse, especially those who were sexually abused, can suppress their traumatic experiences for years, even decades. This is because at the time of the abuse, many survivors were threatened or brainwashed by the perpetrator to conceal the abuse and were made to believe that they were responsible for it. Additionally, recalling the abuse often elicit intense feelings of fear, shame, and self-blame for the survivors. Many survivors make considerable efforts to forget their traumas until they encounter a trigger—imagery portraying sexual assault, a news story about a child victim of molestation, being in a relationship with a significant other, a life event such as the birth of a child, or having their child turn the age they were when they were abused—that causes the memory of the trauma to resurface.

Because many survivors require considerable time to heal before they're able to report the crime, I believe all states should eliminate the statutes of limitations for physical and sexual abuse. While twenty states in our nation allow sexual crimes against children to be adjudicated no matter when they occurred, California was not one of them when I made my reports to law enforcement, the Catholic Church, and the Board of Psychology.

As of January 1, 2020, California's statute of limitations for sexual crimes against children has been extended to age forty (previously age 26) or within five years (previously 3 years) of the discovery of the sexual abuse. This change was made possible by Assembly Bill 218, which was sponsored by Assemblywoman Lorena Gonzales, and signed by Governor Gavin Newsom on October 13, 2019. This bill also gives survivors of sexual abuse, regardless of their age, a three-year window to file claims against their perpetrators and the institutions responsible, regardless of when the abuse occurred. While the bill fell short of eliminating the statute of limitations, it does allow survivors more time and a short window of opportunity to file civil complaints against the perpetrators and hold them accountable for their atrocious crimes.

—— ∞∞∞ ——

On the clear, warm Sunday morning of July 8th, 2001, my dad was sitting and talking to my mom on the couch when he told her to call 911. Then he became mute, slumped to the side, and lost consciousness. My sister Kathy, who was visiting, called 911. Then she called me, saying that my dad had "probably had a stroke" and was being rushed to the emergency room by ambulance.

I immediately told Ladson what had happened, and we grabbed Carina, jumped into the car, and made what felt like the longest drive of my life to the hospital. The drive took over an hour. We told Carina that we were going to see Ong Ngoai (maternal grandfather, in Vietnamese) in the hospital because he was sick.

Once we got there, I held Carina in my arms as I raced into the emergency room. My father appeared unconscious on his hospital bed when I stepped into the room. I said to him in Vietnamese, "Dad, it's Carolee, I'm here with Carina."

There was no response.

Then Carina, who was almost three years old at the time, called out to my dad, "Ong Ngoai! Ong Ngoai! Ong Ngoai has a boo-boo!"

Immediately, my dad sat upright and yelled out, "Ong Ngoai loves Carina!" Then he laid back down and was out again.

Within minutes, Ladson came into the room with the ER doctor. The physician told us that my dad had suffered a large hemorrhagic stroke on the right side of his brain. This type of stroke occurs when a blood vessel ruptures and causes blood to accumulate in the brain. This puts pressure on the brain and causes a loss of blood flow to the surrounding areas, resulting in paralysis on the opposite side of the body. He said if my dad survived the stroke, he would become paralyzed on the left side of his body. For now, all the doctor could do was monitor the bleeding in his brain and hope that the stroke wouldn't kill him.

With heavy hearts, my siblings and I took shifts staying with my dad around the clock at his bedside in the intensive care unit. To prepare for the worst, my mom asked a priest to come and give my dad the last rites. This is a Catholic ritual that prepares the soul of the dying person for death. Then we all prayed, hoping that God would spare my dad's life and not take him away from us so soon.

While keeping vigil at my dad's bedside, my siblings and I tried to minimize his suffering and preserve his dignity. We wrote down everything the nurses and doctors did and told us. We made sure we were there for rounds first thing in the morning to get updates from the doctors and medical staff. We kept each other apprised of everything related to my dad's condition, and tried to convey to everyone on the hospital staff that he was a kind person who was a wonderful husband, father, and grandfather. We brought in pictures of my dad with his children and grandchildren. We felt it was important to humanize him, since objectification of patients is a significant problem in hospital settings and can compromise care. Fortunately, I hadn't yet returned to work at the time and was able to spend a lot of time with my dad.

During one of my shifts two days into his ICU stay, I noticed that my dad's face had turned beet red and he was struggling to breathe. At this point, he hadn't yet regained consciousness from the stroke and was still in danger of dying. I became alarmed and alerted the nurse. She told me that she thought he might be taking his last breaths. Immediately, I insisted that she do something to save him. I inquired whether she had given him something toxic within the last hour, since he seemed fine before this sudden turn for the worse. She checked his chart and discovered that he had been given a medication that contained alcohol. I knew that he'd always had an anaphylactic allergic reaction to alcohol. I immediately informed the nurse of this, and she swiftly gave him an epinephrine shot to reverse the symptoms. After this scare, I requested that the nurse mark his chart in huge bold letters that he was allergic to alcohol.

The following morning, I came into the hospital early and saw that my dad was still unconscious. I was informed by the nurse that they were going to perform brain surgery on him as soon as a surgeon was available.

"Why the sudden change in treatment plan?" I asked. "The doctor told me last night that we'd continue with the wait-and-see approach."

"Your father had a brain scan this morning that showed the bleeding in his brain had increased considerably."

I called Ladson and asked him to talk to my dad's doctor as soon as possible. Ladson discovered that the scan used to make the decision to operate immediately was not his but belonged to another patient. We were quite upset—but relieved that this second medical mistake was detected and the unnecessary brain surgery averted.

My dad survived his stroke, regaining consciousness after a week. He was moved to University of California, San Francisco Medical Center (UCSF), since it was better equipped to deal with stroke patients. He stayed there for an additional three weeks. Again, one of his children was always at his bedside.

After my dad regained consciousness, he retained his ability to talk, but as predicted was paralyzed on the entire left side of his body. From UCSF he was transferred to a facility that specialized in the treatment of stroke patients to begin the process of rehabilitation. It was about an hour from where I lived, and I went there four times a week to be with my dad. Carina was three years old by then, and sometimes I brought her with me. She would sing, talk to him, cheer him on during his physical therapy sessions, and wheel him around in his wheelchair (with my help). Her visits always brightened his day. Because of this we always made the effort to take Carina to see my dad at least once a week. We also made tapes of her singing Vietnamese and American songs so he could listen to them at his leisure.

One day when I was visiting my dad at the center without Carina, I followed him into the physical therapy room. I could see how hard he was working on his recovery: beads of sweat trickled down his forehead and he was panting. I cheered him on and clapped each time he finished a set of exercises. He looked at me after the last repetition of arm exercises and said.

"See Carolee, this is my PhD. I will work hard to regain my strength and mobility like you worked hard to get your doctorate."

My heart swelled with love and admiration for my dad. Here again, when faced with another adversity, my dad took it in stride and showed courage and perseverance.

After seven weeks at the rehab center, my dad was discharged. My mom quit her job as a housekeeper to be his caregiver. With physical therapy, my dad eventually regained his ability to walk, though he needed a cane. Thankfully his speech, attention, concentration, and memory remained intact, and he was able to dress himself and maintain regular activities of daily living such as brushing his teeth, showering, and using the bathroom.

The Tran family at a Hawaiian-themed reunion in 2006.
FRONT ROW: Ryan and Zack (Betty's sons), Dad, and Carina.
MIDDLE ROW: Jane, Betty, Mom, me, Kathy, Elizabeth (Robbie's wife), and Robbie. BACK ROW: Jim (Betty's husband) and Ladson holding Mika.

Neither of my parents ever complained about my dad's stroke or how it had disrupted their lives. They were grateful that he had survived it and focused on the various gifts the stroke brought them. My mom saw it as an opportunity for both of them to retire from physically demanding jobs. She was completely devoted to caring for my dad. At the same time, my dad worked hard to regain his strength and mobility and never whined or felt sorry for himself.

"My stroke showed me how blessed I am to be surrounded by so much love and devotion," Dad told my siblings and me at a family gathering after his return home. "I'm thankful that God gave me more time to be with you. I'm deeply touched and grateful for the love and caring you showed me during my time in the hospital. Even when I was unconscious, I felt your love and dedication. It gave me the will to fight hard to live!"

About a year after Carina was born, Ladson and I had talked about having another child so that Carina could have a sibling. I became pregnant again early in 2000, but had an excruciatingly painful miscarriage after three months. I was urged to go immediately to the ER to get it checked out. Medical tests revealed that I'd had an ectopic pregnancy—where the fertilized egg lodges in the fallopian tube rather than the uterus—a potentially life-threatening condition for the mother. Luckily I didn't require surgery.

Ladson and I kept trying to get pregnant for another year, but we were unsuccessful. My doctor recommended that we see a fertility specialist right away, since I was thirty-five years old at the time and was "in the advanced maternal age category." What followed were months of testing and procedures for Ladson and me, which ultimately yielded a diagnosis of "unexplained infertility."

We discussed the various options: using fertility drugs, intrauterine insemination, in vitro fertilization, and adoption. In the end we concluded that we were grateful to have Carina and would accept God's will.

Then in early April of 2003, I found out I was pregnant again. I'd bought a special baby announcement card for Ladson over a year before and had held onto to it, hoping that I'd have the opportunity to give it to him. That night, Carina and I met Ladson at our favorite Japanese restaurant near his work for dinner. Once we sat down, Carina handed Ladson the card and urged him to open it right away.

The front of the card had a picture of a pair of baby's feet. "Hello Daddy," I'd written inside, "I can't wait to meet you in 9 months. Love, Your baby #2."

Ladson was ecstatic, and the three of us celebrated that night. But our joy quickly turned into concern and sadness when I began bleeding a week later. I braced myself for another miscarriage. Though that didn't happen, my doctor recommended that I go in every couple of days for blood draws to monitor my level of human chorionic gonadotropin (HCG), a hormone that's produced during pregnancy. My HCG levels continued to increase steadily, which was a good sign.

Several weeks later, my doctor ordered an ultrasound to ensure that it wasn't another ectopic pregnancy. The appointment was on a late Friday afternoon, and Ladson was with me. At the beginning of the procedure, the technician was chatty and friendly, explaining to us what he would be doing. First he revealed the good news: I didn't have another ectopic pregnancy. Then he looked worried and glum. He moved the ultrasound wand around multiple times, as if he was searching for something that wasn't there.

I could tell instantly that something was wrong. It turned out that the amniotic sac that was supposed to contain the fetus was empty. There was no baby. My doctor warned me that I should expect the "empty sack" to expel itself from my body over the next several days.

Ladson and I were silent on the drive home. Once we got to the house, I went straight to my room to cry while Ladson paid the babysitter who'd been watching Carina. After the sitter had gone, Carina came into my room and saw that I was crying.

"What's wrong, Mommy?" she asked me.

"Mommy feels sad because the doctor did a test and it showed that there was no baby in my tummy. But don't worry—we'll keep praying for a baby."

That night, I had a dream that was so vivid it felt more like a vision. The Virgin Mary appeared to me. She exuded deep compassion and warmth and spoke to me in a soothing voice. "Don't fret my child. Everything will be okay."

The following morning, I awoke feeling a deep sense of gratitude, calm, and well-being. I prayed to Mother Mary and told her that I felt at peace and would accept whatever was meant to happen. I put my faith in her.

In three weeks, I was due to have another ultrasound to assess the status of the "empty sack." As the days progressed, I continued to feel a sense of equanimity about the whole situation. I sensed in my body and my heart that I was pregnant, in spite of what the ultrasound had revealed.

Then about two weeks after the initial ultrasound, I opened my front door and noticed a small bird's nest burrowed inside the wreath we'd hung there. It contained two perfect tiny white eggs. I had never seen anything like this in my wreath before, nor have I since. I interpreted the eggs as a sign from Mother Mary, letting me know that she was with me and reassuring me that everything would be okay. In the meantime, I continued to pray for strength and acceptance of whatever was meant to be.

Carina also continued to pray daily: "Please God and Mother Mary, please don't let mommy's tummy be an empty sack. Please give us a baby!"

On a late Friday afternoon, exactly three weeks after the first ultrasound, Ladson and I went in for a second look. This time, we saw a healthy fetus with a strongly beating heart! We were elated and beyond grateful.

Carina was over the moon when we came home and showed her the ultrasound picture. From that point forward, she sang and talked to the baby every day. She also started praying fervently for a baby sister. When we found out later that Carina would indeed have a baby sister, she responded with, "Yes! Thank you, Mother Mary for giving me a baby sister! I can't wait to meet her!"

On a cold winter day in 2003, our second daughter, Mikaela Marie was born in the early evening. Her middle name was chosen to honor Mother Mary for her divine intervention. Mika's birth had been particularly challenging because she presented in an occipito posterior position for delivery, where she laid face up rather than face down. When this happens, labor tends to be longer, since the baby has a harder time passing through the birth canal, and it often results in a cesarean section being done. But after three hours of hard pushing, my precious and perfect baby came into the world with a full head of jet-black hair, weighing in at eight pounds six ounces (a fair size considering that I'm only five feet tall). I was again thankful to my body for its strength and determination. Mika's birth was truly a miracle given that she started out as an "empty sack."

Carina met Mika later in the day at the hospital and was a doting big sister from the beginning. I came home with Mika the following day and had Carina help out with the baby. She handed us the diaper wipes whenever we changed Mika's diaper. She also assisted each time we bathed or fed her baby sister. Though Mika was a calm, easy, happy, alert baby, like all babies, she sometimes cried. Whenever she did, Carina always knew the best way to get her to stop—like singing to her or making entertaining noises. This seemed to help them bond with each other—Carina never expressed any feelings of jealousy towards Mika. At the same time, Mika adored her big sister and wanted to copy everything Carina did. Ladson and I felt incredibly grateful and blessed to have two healthy daughters. Now, our family was complete!

CHAPTER 21

Homecomings

On February 1st, 2015, a cold, dreary Sunday morning, I received a phone call from my sister Jane, who is a social worker. She had gone to visit my parents and discovered that my dad was experiencing delirium—seeing things that weren't there, talking rambling nonsense, and not oriented to time or place. Jane told me she was taking my dad to the ER to get checked out. I immediately got into my car and drove to the hospital to meet them there.

Once there, I saw that my dad was indeed in a deep state of confusion. He didn't recognize me and was having visual hallucinations and talking nonsense. His doctor informed me that he had pneumonia, which was caused by the flu, which resulted in the delirium. They were admitting him immediately to the ICU for treatment.

For ten days, my siblings and I took turns staying with my dad around the clock. Again we advocated for him and did our best to minimize his suffering and preserve his dignity. Again we tried to humanize him to his caregivers by telling them about his kindness and what a wonderful husband, father, and grandfather he was. About a week into his hospital stay, he coded (went into cardiac arrest, almost died, and had to be revived). Fortunately, he pulled through but was very frail even after his pneumonia had cleared up. His doctor discharged him to a rehabilitation center on February 10th for additional care and physical therapy. The center was about an hour from where I lived.

I went there four times a week to visit. On Thursday, February 19th, I spent the entire day there with my dad and talked with him at length. It was Tet—Lunar New Year—so I brought special cookies for us to share. I sat holding his warm hand and asked him about his mood and how he was feeling. He said he felt good, was feeling stronger, and was looking forward to our family's Tet celebration in two days. His doctor would provide him with a special pass to come home for the day and celebrate the occasion with us.

My dad also said he was praying to God for strength, so he could be around for all of us, though he also emphasized that he was not afraid to die. "I've had the most blessed life with all of you. I'm ready and willing to leave this earth whenever Our Heavenly Father and Mother Mary tell me it's my time. Death is not a scary thing for me, but more like a homecoming—an opportunity to meet my Maker and to reunite with my loved ones in heaven. The thing I'm most fearful of is being a burden."

I squeezed his hands, looked him in the eyes, and said in Vietnamese, "You will never be a burden. It's an honor and a privilege to take care of you! I'm here for you in the same way that you were there for mom's dad."

He nodded his head and smiled warmly at me, conveying contentment and gratitude.

After lunch, his physical therapist came into his room and announced that it was time for him to do his exercises. He requested that they have the session in the room since he wanted me to see him work out. His therapist relented, saying, "Okay Tom, just this one time."

During this session, he was chatty, proudly pointing out to the therapist the various cards and decorations we had made for him. "Look at how much I'm loved by my kids and grandkids. Aren't those big red hearts, balloons, and cards beautiful! I'm lucky that my kids and grandkids come to see me every day."

From the way he spoke, I could tell that he felt loved by all of us. He seemed so happy, energetic, and filled with gratitude. Later on I said goodbye to him, telling him I would see him in two days for the Tet celebration.

The next day, a Friday evening, February 20th, Ladson and I spoke to my dad via speaker phone. He sounded animated and expressed excitement about coming home the following day.

My dad passed away just one hour after this conversation.

I was stunned and heartbroken by the suddenness of his death. It appeared that he'd had a massive stroke or a heart attack. My dad had turned on the call light, but as soon as the attendant came into the room, my dad took two quick breaths and then passed away.

It seemed he'd died quickly, without pain or suffering. I believe he left this world in a positive state of mind, and I will forever be grateful that I was at the rehab center on that Thursday to hear what he said to the physical therapist and witness the joy, pride, and contentment he felt.

I received many precious gifts from my dad. He taught me to love deeply and give what you can without harming your own well-being. His devotion to others gave him tremendous joy and energy.

He was the president of our Vietnamese community for over twenty-five years, until his stroke. I was astonished by all the lives he had touched. At his wake and funeral, so many people from all walks of life and various faiths talked about his generosity and compassion. Their reflections about him gave me great comfort and reminded me that at the end of the day, what really matters is whether we have been loved, given love, and reached out to help those who are in need.

If we're fortunate enough to experience these three things, we are rich and have lived a full life.

My dad also taught me about the importance of minimizing regrets. When we have fewer regrets, we are freer and are more liberated from deep shame and sadness, which allows us to live our best life. He exemplified this in the earnest and peaceful way he lived his life, whether it was caring for his dying father-in-law, sending money home to Vietnam for his family, fixing cars on cold rainy days, working as a janitor, or carrying out his leadership role in the community. I wonder if his day-to-day intention to minimize regrets contributed to his compassionate, grounded, and serene presence—people often referred to him as The Buddha.

My siblings and I have tried to minimize our regrets by emulating my parents' practice of filial piety towards their parents. We worked as a team to take care of each other while my parents worked outside of the home, assisted my parents at their manual labor jobs when possible, and supported them through their various health crises.

During my dad's last hospitalization and at his death, my siblings and I were a team again. This time, we helped him with his "homecoming"—his journey home to meet his Maker and to reunite with his parents in heaven. While I miss my dad, I'm also filled with deep feelings of gratitude. I know how lucky I was to have him as my father. The heartache of losing him and missing him is coupled with the realization that my grief is really a gift and a blessing. The sorrow I feel reflects the deep love that we shared and the love and devotion he gave to his children and my mom.

———— ∞∞ ————

Exactly four months after my dad passed away, my family experienced another kind of homecoming. Ladson and I took Carina and Mika to Vietnam for the first time. At this point Carina was sixteen years old and Mika eleven. We left for Vietnam on June 20th for a monthlong trip, which began with volunteer work in Ha Noi.

Carina, Mika, and I volunteered at a center that served children with autism spectrum disorders. Carina is affectionate, thoughtful, dramatic, fun-loving, and tends to wear her heart on her sleeve. Mika is also thoughtful but tends to be a little more reserved, even-keeled, and observant; she keeps her thoughts and feelings closer to the vest.

Both of them loved being at the autism center and became completely immersed in their work there. They held, played, and interacted with the children by taking part in their instruction. Carina and Mika held up flashcards of various items and had the children name them. They also took part in one-on-one play therapy with the kids. After a few days of getting to know them, the children responded positively. Carina and Mika learned about the nature of autism spectrum disorder and the patience that is required to work with these precious children.

In Ha Noi, we also went to see my great uncle and his family. He was my mom's paternal uncle who had chosen to stay in the North, and he'd ended up being a communist official. Ladson and I had met him on our first trip back to Vietnam in 1997. He strongly resembled my maternal grandfather and was very warm and loving toward us.

Carina and Mika learned on this visit with my great uncle that people are people. My great uncle's strong affiliation with the communist government didn't make him a "bad person." The Vietnam War was a civil war that tore the country and its families apart, including ours.

After this visit with my great uncle, we traveled onto Hue, Da Nang, and Ha Long Bay. In Hue, the former imperial capital of Vietnam, we toured the Citadel, a stone fortress that housed the royal family during the Nguyen Dynasty and was the military heart of the imperial capital. It protected the royal family and the Vietnamese people from 1802 to 1945. The Citadel was once a luxurious and magnificent city, until most of it was destroyed during the Vietnam War. Hue was the site of one of the longest and bloodiest battles of the war. During the Battle of Hue, which raged from January 30th to March 3rd, 1968, eighteen battalions consisting of South Vietnamese and American soldiers fought and defeated the Viet Cong.

Learning about this history made me miss my dad and gave me a deeper appreciation for the sacrifices he had made as a soldier and the trying conditions he had to fight under. I wished I could have asked him what it was like to fight in the Battle of Hue and how he coped with the fear and danger. Being in the Citadel also made me think about all the Vietnamese and American soldiers who fought in the Vietnam War, especially those who made the ultimate sacrifice of death. It made me sad as I pondered the brutality of war, the suffering, displacement, and cost in human lives.

After this, we went to Da Nang, a coastal city with many beautiful beaches, and one of Vietnam's most important ports. Da Nang was a wonderful place to decompress and relax. We swam in the warm turquoise waters and went to a local restaurant where we picked out various live crustaceans and had them cooked on the spot. Both Carina and Mika are foodies and have always loved trying new things.

Then we headed to Ha Long Bay, which is one of the most magnificent places to see in Vietnam. We took a cruise and were captivated by the emerald water punctuated with numerous limestone pillars jutting up into the sky and the islets spread throughout the bay. On the cruise, we met a large Vietnamese group consisting of many families with their kids. They invited us to join them at the predinner reception and offered us various tropical fruits—jackfruit, longan, and mangosteen. Carina and Mika enjoyed trying the fruits and had a great time talking and taking pictures with the kids. Both girls were impressed by how kind and embracing these families were.

Going to Vietnam with Ladson, Carina, and Mika was an incredibly moving and healing experience for me. It was wonderful to see my daughters soaking up my homeland and culture. They loved how the Vietnamese people were so friendly, generous, and welcoming. They also enjoyed all the regional dishes. In Ha Noi, they had *bun cha* (pork with rice noodle) and lemongrass tofu. In Hue, we had *bun bo Hue* (beef noodle soup) and all agreed that my mom's version was superior.

It was exhilarating to see Ladson and the girls speaking Vietnamese and to witness Carina and Mika embracing their Vietnamese identity in a deeper way. This trip back to Vietnam with my family was a wonderful reminder that I had survived the harrowing escape and realized the American dream. Now I was back with my daughters to introduce them to my beloved motherland.

Our family at Ha Long Bay in Vietnam, in June 2015.

CHAPTER 22

When Hate Descends

On November 9, 2016, I was stunned by Donald Trump's presidential win. It made me wonder whether America had lost its way. I questioned how such a self-serving person, who was filled with so much anger and divisiveness, could be voted into the highest office of the land.

In the days following the election, I found myself feeling frightened and agitated whenever I turned on the news. I was horrified and incensed by Trump's contempt for immigrants and refugees, and his conflation of them with terrorists and criminals. The atmosphere of hostility, intimidation, and inhospitality that he and his administration were generating against immigrants felt not only inhumane, unjust, and racist but also like a personal slap in the face. I was particularly alarmed and outraged by Trump's inhumane treatment of the migrant children—separating them from their parents and putting them in cages. Numerous children, including Felipe Gomez Alonzo and Jakelin Caal Maquin, ages 8 and 7, respectively, died in the care of our government. These children took their last breaths on this earth without having a single family member by their side.

I was consumed with worry for these migrant children and couldn't help but identify with them. I recalled my own escape and the grief and terror I'd felt when I was separated from my family. I shuddered to think what these kids were going through as they were being ripped away from their parents, not knowing whether they'd ever be reunited again. Research has shown that such traumas have short- and long-term adverse effects on children's brains, psychological, physiological, and social development. As I ruminated on the plight of these children, a quote from Dr. Martin Luther King Jr. kept reverberating through my mind: "In the end, we will remember not the words of our enemies, but the silence of our friends."

Dr. King's words gnawed at me and compelled me to do some soul searching. I asked myself what I could do to help these children. I was tired of cycling between feelings of anger, fear, and despair. At the same time, I knew I couldn't be the silent friend—I had to do something! As a refugee, I felt a deep sense of responsibility to rebuke Trump and his administration's attempts to demonize and dehumanize refugees by calling us "invaders," "criminals," and "terrorists." And as a psychologist and a mother, I felt a strong moral and ethical duty to speak out against the harm that was being perpetrated against these innocent children and their families.

To that end, I decided that I would try to help by speaking out more about my experience as a Vietnamese refugee. I would try to humanize who we were and illustrate that we're productive members of society who make valuable contributions to this country. I'd hoped that by sharing my experience, I could cultivate greater compassion and understanding for immigrants and refugees.

As a result, I accepted as many invitations as possible to talk about my refugee experience. I spoke to newspapers, magazines, radio programs, and thousands of college students at various campuses. I believe that these students represent our greatest hopes for the future—they can and do propel the social and political discourse and action of this country towards greater tolerance, justice, and equality. In their classrooms, clubs, and organizations, I spoke about my own and my family's experiences as refugees. I was explicit and undaunted in my criticisms of President Trump and his administration's policies on immigration, their inhumane treatment of migrant families, and their negative portrayals of immigrants. I also stressed to these students the importance of civic and political engagement and urged them to vote in the 2018 midterm elections.

In March of 2017, I received an invitation from Sacramento's public television station, KVIE, to be filmed talking about my escape experience. It would be aired that fall as a companion to Ken Burns's documentary *The Vietnam War*. My story would be a part of a video collection entitled *My Vietnam War Story*. I accepted the request, viewing it as an opportunity to share with the public my and my family's experiences as refugees. I hoped that hearing our story would awaken a shared sense of humanity in others and promote greater empathy for immigrants. An appointment was set for taping at the studio.

On the designated day I went to KVIE. The studio was frigid. This immediately worried me, because I have cold intolerance due to my polio. I also have essential tremor, a nerve disorder that causes uncontrollable shaking in my hands and head. When I'm cold, the tremors can become so severe that it looks like I have Parkinson's disease. I asked them to turn up the heat but was told that the studio needed to be kept cold because the lighting tended to make it too hot. So I didn't fuss and just soldiered on with the taping. I spoke for over an hour about my escape out of Vietnam and the resettlement process for me and my family.

On September 12th, 2017, I spoke at a large KVIE premier event for both Ken Burns's and KVIE's Vietnam documentary series. Two days later, I was interviewed on air by Beth Ruyak, for *Insight,* at Capital Public Radio. The discussion focused on the two documentaries and my experiences as a Vietnamese refugee.

At both events, I talked about the importance of humanizing the face of war by discussing the horror, displacement, and suffering that resulted from them. I thanked the Vietnam veterans for their service to our country and apologized to them for the poor treatment they received upon their return home. I again criticized Trump and his administration's demonization and treatment of migrants. I told the audience that I was there to portray a different image of immigrants and refugees as hardworking, law-abiding citizens who'd had no choice but to flee our homelands due to conditions of war and violence. We escaped in search of refuge and the opportunity to live productive lives—basic things that all humans strive for.

I also urged the audience to think about the plight of the eight hundred thousand Dreamers and their families, who are living in fear and limbo. I implored them to put pressure on Congress to reinstate the Deferred Action for Childhood Arrivals (DACA) Program, and to push for the naturalization of these young people. Finally, I challenged the audience to consider what they would do if war and violence broke out in their own backyard. How would they want the world community to treat them?

Throughout September and October of 2017, my documentary was aired repeatedly by KVIE. The most meaningful part of participating in this project was hearing from the public and learning how my story touched them. Many people called, wrote, and shared that the documentary gave them a deeper understanding and appreciation for immigrants and refugees and their struggles. Shortly after *My Vietnam War Story* was aired, I learned from KVIE that my story was nominated for a regional Emmy. While it didn't end up winning, it was an honor to be nominated.

On the beautiful Sunday afternoon of September 24th, 2017, I had just returned home from a rejuvenating weekend with my soul sisters, my girlfriends from college. We've been friends for thirty-five years and have been there for each other through thick and thin. Regardless of what's happening in our lives, we make it a point to spend at least one weekend together each year. On these trips, we get caught up, share parenting tips, exchange good book titles, and enjoy wonderful meals together. This year, we went up to the mountains near Lake Tahoe, California.

After arriving home and saying a quick hello to Ladson, Carina, and Mika, I went to the gym. I usually exercise five times a week as a general routine for self-care. After my workouts, I always go to the gym's outdoor hot tub as my reward. I use this quiet time to meditate and get relief for my chronic aches and pain, remnants from the polio.

Five minutes into my relaxing soak, I heard a splash. An older Caucasian man stepped into the hot tub. I'll refer to him as John. We made eye contact and exchanged smiles. Then I closed my eyes again and returned to my meditation. Within a minute he said, "Are you meditating? You look like you're meditating."

I nodded my head and said nothing. Then John proceeded to tell me that he'd heard from another club member that I'd lived in Boston at one point. He launched into talking about "the Boston bomber," how "his family should've never been let into this country," and how "all refugees were frauds and should be sent back." I should mention that even though I had seen John at the club several times, I had never exchanged more than a few cursory words with him, nor had I ever told him anything about myself.

I opened my eyes and said flatly, "I don't think all refugees should be sent back. Please don't talk to me, I'm meditating." Then I closed my eyes again.

John ignored my request and proceeded to tell me in a loud voice how he "hated all Blacks and Hispanics," how "they're all criminals" and "commit most of the crimes, and that's why prisons are full of them!"

I didn't respond. At the same time, another man had joined us in the hot tub. I was relieved and had hoped that John would shift his attention to the newcomer. Instead John raised his voice and said, "Hey, are you listening? Did you hear what I'd just said?"

I stayed silent. Then John yelled, "You're a refugee, aren't you? I know you are!"

The contempt in John's voice sent a chill up my spine. I wondered how he knew that I was a refugee and why he was bringing this up. I opened my eyes and saw John glaring at me. I told him again that I didn't want to talk.

Then John began to scream. "You probably read shit like the *New York Times,* don't you! It drives me fuckin' crazy that you imbeciles can't think for yourselves!"

I stood up, looked him in the eye, and spoke in a calm but firm voice: "You need to stop *right now*, or I'll report you for harassment!"

"No, you need to educate yourself, bitch. Think for yourself, bitch!"

I looked at the other man in the tub.

"Did you hear what he just called me?"

The man shook his head, averted his gaze, and said nothing.

The bystander's passive and indifferent response seemed to embolden John further to escalate his angry tirade. He screamed expletives at me, calling me the most demeaning and vile names, while I repeatedly told him to stop.

After about five minutes of his persistent vitriol, I stepped out of the hot tub and headed for the dressing room, while he continued to shout obscenities at me. Once I stepped into the ladies' locker room, I found that it was empty. At this point I was on high alert. My heart was pounding and my mind racing. I wondered whether John was going to barge into the dressing room and continue his angry rant. I tried to think about what I would do if he did. *Would I scream for help? What if no one hears me? I have to hurry up and get out of here!*

I quickly got into one of the bathroom stalls, locked the door, and changed as fast as I could. As I was coming out of the stall, a woman I'd never met before came into the room and inquired with concern, "Are you okay? I heard how he went off on you. You were awesome in how you stood up to him. He was so aggressive! I was afraid he was going to put his hands on you."

I was grateful that the woman had come to check on me. She felt like an angel sent by God and Mother Mary to help me. I thanked her for her kindness and asked her for her name and phone number. I told her that I wanted to report John to the owner and would appreciate it if I could have her as a witness. She told me her name (I'll call her Stacey), and said that she would be happy to assist in any way. Stacey and I went to the front desk and reported the incident to a staff member. Then I went home.

Once I got home I told Ladson, Carina, and Mika about what had occurred and then went straight to my computer to write down everything about the incident while it was still fresh in my mind.

At the time, Carina and Mika were nineteen and fourteen years old, respectively. Ladson and I were disappointed and saddened that our daughters were being touched by the reality of racism—directed at their mother, and in their own hometown. We'd moved to this city thinking that such things wouldn't happen to us here, given its reputation as a progressive college town. We were wrong.

As a family we'd had many discussions about issues related to race and social justice at the dinner table. That night, we talked about how bigotry was a problem in our society, how racism was in the air, how unfortunate it was that certain racial ethnic and religious groups were more burdened by it compared to others, and how we all have a responsibility to speak out against it.

"Are you going to quit going to the gym for a while?" the kids asked me.

"No," I told them. "We must never let people like John intimidate us or change how we go about living our lives."

I told them that I was reporting John to the police and the gym owner the following day. If John tried to do anything, I would use the full the extent of the law to prosecute him. Ladson wondered whether John might have seen my documentary on KVIE and targeted me as a result.

After dinner, I checked my work phone and saw that I'd received four text messages from a number I didn't recognize at 8:24 p.m. When I opened them, I saw at once that it was John who had sent these texts. They contained articles, graphs, and numbers of incarceration rates in California by race. In his message, John said that he was sending me this information to "educate" me and "prove" that "most crimes in America are committed by Blacks and Hispanics."

Getting the texts from John upset me; I felt like he was invading my personal space. I told Ladson about the texts and then went back to our room to meditate, something I do every night before bed. As I sat on my meditation cushion, my dad's words came back to me: "Nobody can hurt me with their ignorant and hateful words and actions. Their behaviors say more about who they are than who I am."

My dad had said this to me years before when I told him I was scared for him, at a time when he was a victim of multiple acts of racial hate. He'd held his head high and didn't let people's ignorance and venom affect him. Now his sage words provided me with great comfort and grounding as I encountered my own experience of racism.

Immediately after breakfast the following morning, I went to the gym and spoke to the owner, whom I'll refer to as Sheri, about what had happened the night before. I read to her my account of the incident and gave her a copy. I also gave her Stacey's contact information, since she was a witness. Sheri told me she would look into the matter and talk with me after my workout.

When I met up with her later, Sheri expressed regret and concern for what had happened to me. She then called John while I was in her office to tell him that his membership had been terminated. At first John tried to deny everything. He said that "we were just talking." When Sheri told him that there were witnesses who reported him, he screamed and verbally threatened her. After Sheri got off the phone with John, she filed a police report, told her staff to be extra vigilant, and instructed them to call 911 if he came into the gym. She also relayed to me that the police had advised me to go to the police station right away to "file a hate crime report."

I left the gym and went straight to the police station. I was greeted by Officer Tim (not his real name), and he led me into a windowless room. I read him what I'd written about the incident and told him what had transpired with Sheri at the gym that morning, including that the officer she'd spoken with had instructed me to come in and file a hate crime report. I told Officer Tim that John's racists comments and his rage concerned me. I wanted to know what I could do to protect myself given that he had already sent me four text messages.

Officer Tim, who appeared to be in his early thirties, had a cold facial expression and spoke without emotion in a flat monotone voice. "This isn't a crime. He didn't do anything illegal. He's entitled to his first amendment rights and can say whatever he wants. For it to be a crime, he has to cause you grave bodily harm or threaten immediate danger to your life. Also, your number is published, so he's free to text you as much as he wants. If you don't want that to happen, you have to take steps to remove your number."

"So there's nothing I can do to protect myself?"

"No, there isn't."

I was stunned and stared silently at the officer.

Then I said. "I'm confused as to why another officer from this station just told me to come file a police report immediately if what you're saying is true."

Officer Tim let out a big sigh and replied, "I guess you can fill out a hate incident report if you want."

"Yes," I replied immediately. "Yes, I definitely want to do that."

He asked me to give him my printed account of the incident. Then he stood up abruptly and escorted me out.

"Can I get a copy of the report once it's completed?"

"I don't know how you can do that or how that works."

"Can I talk to someone who does?"

"Go see someone else," he said, "up front."

Then he walked quickly out of the room.

———— ✠ ————

I left the police station feeling stunned, frustrated, and angry. I was dismayed by how Officer Tim treated me. It gave me a better appreciation for why some victims may choose to not report crimes committed against them, and empathy for those who report feeling retraumatized by the negative treatment they receive from law enforcement.

One of my friends asked my permission to consult with a trusted city council member, who was also her friend, to inquire whether what had occurred with the officer was appropriate. The council member promptly emailed me and connected me with the chief of police. To his credit, the chief reached out to me and invited me to talk with him in person about the incident. I thanked him for his responsiveness and set up a time to meet with him the following week.

On the designated day, once the chief's secretary had escorted me into his office, I thanked him for meeting with me. I shared details of the hate incident, and consulted with him on how to proceed. He was kind and offered helpful suggestions. He told me that if John texted me again, I should send a message back immediately: "Don't text me again. You're harassing me." Then I should report the incident to the police right away, and they would "take care of the situation." The chief clarified the difference between reporting a hate crime versus filing a hate incident report. What happened to me was a hate incident, and it was good that I had alerted the police and filed a report. The chief also shared that there had been a significant increase in the number of hate crimes and hate incidents committed in our city since the 2016 election.

I brought up with the chief the details of what had happened with Officer Tim. I told him that the officer's interaction with me felt insensitive, dismissive, and blaming. I expressed my concern that such behaviors could traumatize victims who tried to report crimes and discourage victims from coming forward altogether. I thanked the chief for explaining the difference between a hate crime and a hate incident and inquired why Officer Tim didn't tell me I could file a report until the very end and why he seemed to want to discourage me from doing so. The chief apologized to me for what happened and assured me that he would "coach Officer Tim to make the needed changes."

I also suggested sensitivity training for his officers given what happened to me and some recent skirmishes between the police and members of our community. The chief said that his officers received sensitivity training on a regular basis, but perhaps it was time for a refresher course.

The hate incident at the gym was eye-opening and shook me to my core. I had never been spoken to in that way in my whole life by an adult, nor had I ever had such vitriol directed at me. The incident made me wonder whether Trump's rhetoric of white resentment and his demonization of migrants was emboldening people like John to target immigrants.

John and others who think like him have never bothered to learn the truth about our nation's crime statistics. In terms of the numbers of crimes committed, Whites actually commit more crimes in the U.S. than any other ethnic group—which is only logical, given that they make up the majority of the population. The overrepresentation of African Americans and Hispanics in prisons can be attributed to the racial biases inherent in our law enforcement and judicial systems, which tend to pull over (with traffic stops), arrest, convict, and incarcerate these groups at a significantly higher rate, and give them longer sentences, for the same crimes committed by White offenders. Moreover, research over the past twenty years has shown a 130 percent increase in drug crimes committed by Whites, compared to a 50 percent decrease in such crimes committed by Blacks. At the same time, for similar drug offenses, Whites are more likely to receive rehabilitation services such drug treatment, while Blacks are more likely to be sent to prison. Finally, research reveals that immigrants consistently commit significantly fewer crimes than native-born Americans.

These compelling statistics should give all of us pause and compel us to confront those who call immigrants and people of color criminals. We also need to advocate for more equal treatment of all offenders under the law, regardless of race. Given the staggering rates of imprisonment in our country compared to other developing countries, it also would be helpful to invest more money into programs that focus on rehabilitating first-time nonviolent offenders rather than sending them to prison. Those who are incarcerated could benefit from more programs that focus on skills-building, affect regulation, and job training to help prepare them for life outside of prison. For example, prisons that provide mindfulness-based stress reduction and meditation programs to inmates have found them to be very effective and helpful.

Of course, Trump's rhetoric of hate towards immigrants has affected more than just the city I live in. It has coincided with the proliferation of hate groups and a significant increase in hate crimes across America. The Southern Poverty Law Center reported that in 2018, the number of hate groups in America rose to its highest level in twenty years. These groups were responsible for killing at least forty people in the U.S. and Canada in 2018, doubling the number from the year before. Statistics from the FBI for 2017 showed a 30 percent increase in hate crime, and the Anti-Defamation League has revealed that white supremacists and other far-right groups committed the majority of extremist-related murders in the U.S. in 2017.

Trump's refusal to condemn white supremacists for their racist rhetoric and crimes, was illustrated by his reluctance to disavow the support of David Duke (a former Ku Klux Klan Grand Wizard) when he ran for president. His "very fine people on both sides" comment after the Unite the Right rally in Charlottesville, Virginia, where counterprotester Heather Heyer was killed, and his description of Haiti and African countries as "shitholes," are examples of his bigotry and tacit support of hate groups to continue their atrocious activities. In fact, many white supremacists chant his name at their rallies and identify him as a supporter of their causes. The anti-immigrant frenzy fueled by Trump, with talks of migrant caravans "invading" our borders, motivated a white nationalist to murder eleven worshippers in 2018 at The Tree of Life Synagogue in Pittsburg, Pennsylvania, as well as the man who took twenty-two lives in El Paso in 2019. The suspect in the New Zealand shooting, who killed fifty Muslims at two mosques in March of that same year, praised Trump and highlighted him as "a symbol of renewed white identity and common purpose."

Moreover, the ease and frequency with which this president lies, along with his impulsivity, pettiness, and lack of ethics, are deeply troubling. His treatment of women is equally deplorable—objectifying them by making crude comments about their looks, calling them demeaning nicknames, and bragging about sexually harassing them. These behaviors are particularly appalling when one considers that he's supposed to be a role model for others.

Trump and his administration's scapegoating of Muslims, Mexicans, migrants, and nonwhite immigrants is disrespectful, dehumanizing, and dangerous. We have a dark history in this country of marginalizing certain groups so we can deny them their basic rights: women, to deny them the right to vote (among others); Native Americans, to strip them of their land and culture; African Americans, to deny them rights of every kind, both before and after Emancipation; Japanese Americans, who were interned and had their property confiscated during World War II; interracial couples, whose marriages were not legal until 1967; and LGBTQ individuals, to deny them the rights to love, marry, have children, and serve in the military and other occupations.

As has been widely reported, the Trump administration is violating the rights of thousands of migrant children by illegally detaining them for months at a time. It may take two years before these kids are reunited with their families again. Some may never be reunited. Federal law and a 1997 court agreement known as *Flores* require that these children be released to sponsors in the U.S. within twenty days, in most cases. Knowing this current atrocious mistreatment of the migrant children and America's dark past history, we all need to do our utmost to expose and speak out against all forms of injustice, hate, and bigotry. We can't allow America's ugly past to repeat itself in the here and now. Let us heed Dr. Martin Luther King Jr.'s words and not be the silent friend.

I also implore all Americans and the world community to get involved and maximize our efforts to assist refugees worldwide. Perhaps we can begin by showing them compassion rather than demonizing them. Every minute, there are twenty refugees in the world who are displaced because of war, and over half a million are denied access into safe haven countries. As I write this, thousands of Venezuelan refugees are fleeing on foot because of the political crisis that has ensued in their country.

I fervently believe that at the end of the day, it is our humanity, our activism, and our basic acts of kindness towards one another that provide us with the most powerful medicine to heal our racial, political, and social wounds, and to make our world a better place.

CHAPTER 23

Speaking My Truth

In August of 2017, I received an email out of the blue from Father D's sister-in-law on my work address. I'll refer to her as Bea. I had met her over thirty-five years before, when she came to the U.S. for a visit. Given that Bea and I had not maintained contact through the years, I was surprised to hear from her.

In a lengthy message, Bea explained that Father D was in bad health and wanted "urgently to make contact with old friends." He had asked her to find and reach out to me. Bea shared that Father D was at a rehab center recovering from heart surgery and was on dialysis. She indicated that he had left the priesthood many years before, and in 2000 had married a woman who died just two years later from cancer. Bea left me his contact information and urged me to contact him. I wrote Bea back to thank her for the update about Father D and told her that I would pray for him. But I did not reach out to him.

Two weeks later, I received a voicemail from Father D on my work number. In a faint, weak voice he identified himself, left his phone number at the rehab center, and asked, "Please call me. I need to talk to you."

It was strange and startling to hear his voice again after twenty-nine years. I told Ladson about the message, and we discussed whether I should return Father D's call.

"It's your decision, Carolee," he told me. "I'll support whatever you choose to do."

I contemplated Father D's motives for contacting me. I wondered whether he was close to death and was reaching out to apologize for molesting me. I asked myself whether I would regret not returning his call once he was gone. Even though I didn't owe him anything, I didn't have the heart to refuse his request. I believe in the power of redemption and exercising one's humanity, even if Father D didn't deserve it.

At the end, I decided that I would call him back to give him the opportunity to apologize, thinking that it would provide him with some peace, especially if he was dealing with end-of-life issues. I told Ladson that I wanted him in the room with me when I spoke with Father D.

I waited a week before making the call. I wanted to give myself time to reflect on what I would say and to prepare myself psychologically. For years, I had thought about the possibility of having this very conversation with Father D. I fantasized about confronting him and the various questions I would ask him. Now that the opportunity had finally arrived, I felt ready, but apprehensive.

With Ladson by my side, I picked up the phone and dialed Father D's number at the rehab center. The phone rang and rang, but no one picked up. I hung up the phone and thought, *I guess it wasn't meant to be. At least I tried.*

Then a week later, Father D left another message on my work number. He said he had been discharged from the rehab center and was convalescing at home. He left his home number on the message. This time, with more urgency in his voice, he said, "Please Carolee, I beg you, please call me back. I really need to talk to you as soon as possible!"

Again I waited a few days before calling.

On October 8th, 2017, a Sunday afternoon, with Ladson again by my side, I picked up the phone and dialed Father D's home number.

189

As I touched each succeeding digit, I could feel the anticipation rise in my body. I felt flushed, my shoulders tensed up, and my pulse quickened. I could hear the pounding of my heart as it merged with the ringing of Father D's phone. At the end of the second ring, he answered. "Hello."

I was struck by how familiar his voice sounded to me. He sounded strong, confident, warm—just like the old Father D I'd known twenty-nine years before. The warmth in his voice was disarming and transported me back in time, to the countless times I'd spoken to him as a girl. The cordiality of the moment felt so familiar and enticing that I found myself becoming more relaxed and engaged.

I began by expressing my condolence for the death of his late wife. Then I asked why he wanted to talk to me. He claimed that it was Bea's idea and he was under the impression that it was I who wanted to talk with him. That did not make sense, but I didn't bother debating the point. Instead I launched the conversation by asking, "Since I have you on the phone, can you tell me your thoughts about our relationship and what happened between us?"

He replied, "I'm sorry that our relationship ended so soon. I wish it could have gone on longer."

I asked him, "What is your understanding of our relationship, given that you were a grown man and I was thirteen years old when I met you?"

Father D explained that initially he saw me as "a friend" but then, over time, he "fell in love" with me. He said that "we were in love with each other," but he was "90 percent" and I was "10 percent responsible for the relationship."

"There's no way I was responsible for the relationship. You sexually violated me during the camping trip, held me hostage, and ordered me not to tell anyone."

I asked him how he could think that what we had was "a love relationship" in light of the fact that he forced himself on me and threatened me.

"I had a dark side that got unleashed."

"Why didn't you unleash your dark side on an adult woman rather than a child? You violated me, stole my innocence, and traumatized me."

I proceeded to tell him how the molestation caused me to have nightmares and other PTSD symptom for decades, and how I needed years of therapy to deal with the effects of the abuse. After hearing this, Father D said, "I'm sorry for the pain you experienced. The relationship was something that just happened. From what you're saying, I guess you're only 1 percent responsible for the relationship."

I was outraged by his refusal to take full responsibility, so I pressed him: "How can you say the relationship 'just happened'? It went on for seven years! You groomed me, molested me, manipulated me, and threatened me to keep quiet or God would send me and my family to hell. You carried on and abused your power for as long as you could! The abuse would have gone on longer if I didn't leave. What you did was *evil!* You need to take 100 percent responsibility for what happened! I'm not responsible for any of it!"

I went on to express my disgust that he had molested me while being our priest and psychologist. I asked him how, as a psychologist, he could tell me that I was partially responsible for the abuse. Was this what he told his clients who were sexually abused? I told him that as a psychologist, I found him to be despicable in the way he molested me and carried on multiple relationships with various members of our family. I emphasized that he failed in all the moral, ethical, and lawful standards as a priest, a psychologist, and a human being.

Father D said he was sorry for what happened and asked what he could do to make things better. I told him I wanted a written letter of apology from him; it would help me to heal. I told him I had no intention of litigating the matter. In response, he said he would not write a letter. "If my words of apology aren't enough, no letter would suffice."

His condescending words offended me.

"You are a coward! Your words of apology are hollow. Don't you dare infantilize me and tell me what I do and don't need to heal. I'm a grown woman who knows what she wants and needs. I'm not the same child you manipulated years ago! Stop making excuses to avoid taking responsibility for your disgusting acts! Your refusal to write me a letter of apology says a lot about your character, how pathetic you are that you can't even carry out one simple act to make amends for all the harm you've done. I really want you to think about what a coward you are."

"You're right," he said, "sometimes I am cowardly."

Then I confronted him about molesting my sister. He denied the whole thing and expressed anger at her for lying.

"Are you the one who reported me to the police?" he asked. I said yes.

"You betrayed me!" he said angrily.

"Don't you dare make yourself out to be the victim! You were the one who perpetrated all the harm and pain! You are evil and disgusting for violating my sister and me. That's why I had to report you to the police. I had to protect other children from you! Did you forget that you were still practicing as a psychologist and had access to kids? Think about how you betrayed me and my family. Do you know how devastated my parents were when they found out that you molested their daughters? Your evil deeds caused great harm to everyone in my family!"

"I understand why you had to report me to the police. I guess I would do the same thing if I were you," he conceded.

After about an hour, I wrapped things up.

"I'm disappointed that you can't take full responsibility for what you did and your refusal to write a letter of apology. You sound to me like all those pedophiles who refuse to take responsibility for harming their victims. I think you should reconsider writing me a letter of apology, but I thank you for the academic mentoring you provided me throughout high school."

There was a long pause. Then he said, "I'll consider your request," and hung up.

Afterwards, Ladson held me and told me he was proud of me. An incredible sense of relief and lightness swept over me, as if a huge weight had been lifted off of me. Speaking my truth and confronting Father D felt both liberating and empowering. My conversation with him gave me closure on the most painful chapter of my life. I was thankful for the sequence of events that made this moment possible.

I was also grateful to Ladson, my partner for all seasons. Over twenty-six years before, when I'd first told him about my relationship with Father D, Ladson promised me that he would stay by side to support me through everything. Since then, he has been a constant and compassionate companion on my journey of healing. I was struck by the transformative power of love. Even though I'd been able to get away from Father D, that by itself did not end my suffering from the abuse. The thing that brought me true healing was love—developing the capacity to love myself and Ladson's love for me. It's amazing to realize that with great love all things are made possible.

For those of us who have experienced any kind of adversity, including trauma, it's important to get support and treatment so we can heal. Healing can mean different things to different people. For me, it has meant the ability to see the totality of my experiences with clarity, to bear witness to all that has happened to me, to mourn, to cultivate loving-kindness towards myself, to recognize my own resilience, and to live a meaningful and joyful life.

When we seek support, we show that we have courage and the desire to heal. When we go through the healing process, we discover that the gift of trauma and adversity is the realization that we are strong, that we can heal from the horrible things that have happened to us, and that we can survive and thrive in spite of them.

There is an interesting paradox to trauma. Although traumatic events are difficult, they also both force and allow us to uncover our own inner strengths and resourcefulness. We discover that the trauma did not destroy us. The fact that we are still here is a testament to our survival, tenacity, and resiliency. Thus the gift of trauma is resilience.

Our traumas can also give us greater compassion for ourselves and others, fuel our passions for meaningful work, and enhance our efforts and ability to help others. As a psychologist, I know that going through my own traumas and getting professional help to heal from them have made me a better therapist and an ardent advocate for others. For over twenty years I've had the honor and privilege of accompanying many clients through their journeys of healing. Each journey has been sacred, powerful, and inspiring.

The other gift of trauma and healing from it is gratitude. Realizing that each of us has the capacity to heal from pain and deep wounds engenders in us a sense of gratitude towards others who have been there to help us. It is crucial to reach out to others for support, even if it is just one or two trusted individuals. The burden of carrying the pain and secret of our traumas alone can be toxic to our physical and mental health as well as to our sense of self. Speaking about our traumas, when we're ready, can be an extremely healing and liberating experience. I'm truly grateful for the help I've received from the four therapists I've seen through the years as well as the support of friends, family members, and audiences who have shown their love and support by bearing witness. Sharing my own refugee story in the *My Vietnam War Story* documentary was empowering and meaningful. Now I've taken another step on my journey of healing by revealing my story as a survivor of priest sexual abuse. I hope this book will inspire others to reach out for help and embark on their own journeys of healing.

In spite of all I've been through, I'm still an eternal optimist. I've seen from my own experience and witnessed in my work as a psychologist that most people who have suffered traumas can live meaningful, productive, and happy lives if they get adequate support. This gives me hope for the human race, and reminds me that we are resilient, resourceful, and have the capacity to overcome great adversity.

Epilogue

In December of 2017, I was corresponding by email with a wise and trusted mentor I've known for over twenty-five years. She is an accomplished professor and author who was writing to announce the publication of another book. I wrote back to congratulate her, and said in passing that I wanted to write a book about my life but didn't have the time, given everything I was doing.

Within the hour, I got a reply from her: "Carolee, you know you don't have all the time in the world, just get started *now*! There is no perfect time to write a book."

Her words felt like a kick in the pants. I knew that she was absolutely right. I didn't have all the time in the world. I'd better get writing!

As thoughts about the book swirled around in my head, two quotes kept coming to me:

So long as space and beings remain, I will remain in order to help, to serve, and to make my contribution.
—BODHISATTVA VOW

The greatest good is what we do for one another.
—MOTHER TERESA

These quotes have always inspired me and have been the guiding light in my life and work. My desire to make a small contribution towards decreasing suffering in the world and my wish to find ways to transform my adversities into meaningful efforts to help others has been my impetus for writing this book.

So on a cold morning in February of 2018, I sat at my desk to write the first words of my book—to speak my truth about the life I've lived and the things that have happened to me. To the right of my computer I placed the silver dog tag that I wore during my escape out of Vietnam and my father's dog tag, which he wore during the war, fighting in countless battles. These objects that once represented fear, uncertainty, and danger, now give me comfort and remind me of my own and my family's strength and resilience. They symbolize for me the power of the human spirit to survive and thrive under the most difficult of circumstances. I keep them on my desk to inspire me as I write.

I write to pay homage to my parents and grandparents. I write so my kids can know their family history. I write to take another step forward on my journey of healing. But most of all, I write with the deep hope that my story will be of benefit to others.

My dad's dog tags and mine. My baptismal name, Maria,
is shown on the tag along with my Vietnamese name.

Acknowledgments

First and foremost, my deepest gratitude goes to my husband, Ladson Hinton, for being my partner for all seasons—a compassionate companion on my journey of healing, a dedicated and loving father to our daughters, and my fiercest supporter in all my pursuits. Thank you for being my rock, for reading *every single* draft of this book, and for helping me get to the finish line.

To my daughters, Carina and Mika, for their loving support and encouragement. You are my life's greatest blessings, the music in my world, and my hope for the future. This book was written so you may know your family history and your remarkable ancestors.

To my mom for her courage, resilience, and willingness to recall the past so this book could be written. Thank you for having the foresight to escape Vietnam with dad's journals.

To my late father for his perseverance, loving kindness, and bravery, and for always writing, so his words can live on beyond his death.

To my siblings and their families for always standing by me and encouraging me in all my endeavors: Betty Tran-Redman (Jim, Zack, and Ryan Redman), Jane, Kathy, and Robert Tran (Elizabeth, Morgan, and Maddie).

To my in-laws for their support through the years: Mary Drevdahl, Darlene and Ladson Hinton III, Devon Hinton (Susan, Kendra, and Devon Hinton Jr.), Alex Hinton (Nicole Cooley, Meridian and Arcadia Hinton-Cooley), Amanda Lazare, and Elinore Olsen.

ACKNOWLEDGMENTS

To my ancestors for their strength and blessings. I also thank my extended family for helping to raise me, especially to my aunts Annie, Lucy, and Terry Ho for providing the details of their escapes.

To my editors Alan Rinzler and Leslie Tilley for their keen eyes, helpful suggestions, and efficiency.

To the incredibly talented and dedicated team that made the publication of this book a reality: Laura Duffy, Karen Minster, and Ladson Hinton.

To Richard Bromfield, PhD; Trinh Do; Satsuki Ina, PhD; and Arthur Kleiman, MD, for reading early drafts of this book and offering invaluable advice.

To my friends, whose encouragement and belief in me made it possible to complete this book, and whose love and support have made the good times more joyful and the bad times more manageable: Lisa Baumeister, Emily Bay, Lori and Ron Bruno, Gina and Johnnie Caston, Dan and Mitty Dykstra, Josh Fenton, Abbey and Tim Fuete, Kim Hall, Maria Hayashi, Cannie Hertz, Dawn Huetter, Maria and Tom Johnson, Lisa Leavitt, Randy Lee, Angie Miner, Vicki Nagano, Lan Nguyen, Mai Nguyen, Thai and Tu Nguyen, Quyen Tiet, Kieu-Linh Caroline Valverde, Stacey White, Roy Wong, and Jane Yeun.

To my colleagues for their moral and professional support through the years: Lynn Bufka, PhD; Terry Cochetti, MFT; Catherine Cohen, PsyD; Sheryl Fairchild, PhD; Mark Foster, PhD; Scott Anderson; Sara Hoffschmidt, PhD; Melissa Holland, PhD; Loriene Honda, PhD; Laura Katz, PhD; Iko Miyazaki, MFT; Toby Momtaz; Jann Murray-Garcia, MD, MPH; Ju Hee Park, PhD; and Quyen Tiet, PhD.

To the authors who generously took the time to offer me advice about the literary world and provided encouragement: Norbert Bufka, Nicole Cooley, Karen Fowler, Dianne Hales, Huong Nguyen, Viet Thanh Nguyen, and Hoang Chi Truong.

ACKNOWLEDGMENTS

To the Buddhist teachers whose valuable teachings sparked my capacity to see more clearly and positively transformed my life in countless ways: Sylvia Boorstein, PhD; Tara Brach, PhD; the Dalai Lama; Daniel Goleman, PhD; Joan Halifax, PhD; Jon Kabat-Zinn, PhD; Jack Kornfield, PhD; Kristen Neff, PhD; Pema Chodron; Sogyal Rinpoche; Elinore Rosch, PhD; Sharon Salzberg; Shunryu Suzuki; and Thich Nhat Hanh.

To my mentors from Boston University, Harvard Medical School at Massachusetts Mental Health Center, San Francisco General Hospital, and the Vietnamese Youth Development Center for their extraordinary teaching, encouragement, guidance, and kindness: Bart Aoki, PhD; David Belton, PhD; Leslie Brody, PhD; Richard Bromfield, PhD; Jean Lau Chin, EdD; Nang Du, MD; Carol Goodenough, MSW; Jessica Henderson-Daniels, PhD; Davis Ja, PhD; Nazli Kibria, PhD; Evelyn Lee, EdD; Louella Lee; Michael Lyons, PhD; Kathleen Malley-Morrison, PhD; Christopher Morse, PhD; Clare O'Callaghan, EdD; Gary Pfeifer, PhD; June Wolf, PhD; and especially to Mariko Sakurai, PhD, for insisting that this book be written.

My family and I are deeply grateful to the Christian Reform Church for sponsoring us, especially the two families who took us in and gave us shelter.

My deep appreciation to the brave men and women who serve in the United States Armed Forces, as well as their families. In particular, thank you to the American and Vietnamese Vietnam veterans, whose service, sacrifice, and courage were not adequately acknowledged.

I owe a great debt to the four psychologists who walked with me on my journey of healing. Their compassion, guidance, and expertise helped me to heal and enabled me to live a fuller and more meaningful life.

And last but not least, to my clients through the years, for the honor and privilege of accompanying them on their journeys of healing and self-growth. They are a testament to the capacity of the indomitable human spirit to survive and thrive under the most difficult of circumstances.

Made in the USA
San Bernardino, CA
04 June 2020

72694834R00132